T0152815

In Praise of Prejudice

In Praise of Prejudice

The Necessity of Preconceived Ideas

Theodore Dalrymple

Brief Encounters

Encounter Books · New York · London

First edition published in 2006 by Encounter Books,
an activity of Encounter for Culture and Education, Inc.,
a nonprofit, tax exempt corporation.

Encounter Books website address: *www.encounterbooks.com*

Manufactured in the United States and printed on acid-free paper.
The paper used in this publication meets the minimum requirements of
ANSI/NISO Z39.48−1992 (R 1997) (Permanence of Paper).

FIRST EDITION

LIBRARY OF CONGRESS CATALOGING-IN-PUBLICATION DATA

Dalrymple, Theodore.
In praise of prejudice : the necessity of preconceived ideas /
Theodore Dalrymple.
p.   cm.
Includes bibliographical references and index.
ISBN-13: 978-1-59403-202-8 (hardcover : alk. paper)
ISBN-10: 1-59403-202-5 (hardcover : alk. paper)
1. Prejudices--Philosophy. I. Title.
BF575.P9D35 2007
170—dc22
2007024598

10 9 8 7 6 5 4 3

Contents

To the memory of Peter Bauer

He said, "Macaulay, who writes the account of St. Kilda, set out with a prejudice against prejudice, and wanted to be a smart modern thinker; and yet affirms for a truth [what everyone already knows], that when a ship arrives there all the inhabitants are seized with a cold."

James Boswell, *Life of Johnson*
A.D. 1768, Aetat 59

Starting from unlimited freedom I arrive at unlimited despotism.

Fyodor Dostoyevsky, *The Devils*

1 | Prejudice Is Wrong, So Lack of Prejudice Is Right

THESE DAYS, there is a strong prejudice against prejudice: and this is exactly as it should be, is it not? For what is prejudice, if not wholly reprehensible? According to the *Oxford Shorter Dictionary*, prejudice is:

> a previous judgement, especially a premature or hasty judgement. Preconceived opinion; bias favourable or unfavourable; prepossession . . . usually with unfavourable connotation. An unreasoning predilection or objection.

It follows, does it not, that we should strive to be entirely without prejudice?

The archetypical prejudice is that which relates to race. Indeed, the word race and prejudice go together like Mercedes and Benz, or Dolce and Gabbana. It is difficult to say exactly when this association formed, and certainly there was talk of race prejudice before the Nazis changed our moral outlook and priorities, if not forever (for who can see that far into the future?), at least for a long time to come. To hate, despise, depreciate, or discriminate against someone merely because he belongs to a certain racial group now seems to us the worst of all possible vices. This has helped to create a moral climate in which the expression of virtuous, and the abjuration of vicious, sentiment is mistaken for, or taken as the whole of, virtue itself. Let a man be an unscrupulous villain, so long as he utters the right phrases: that is to say, is not prejudiced.

No unprejudiced person, however, could deny the significance of racial prejudice in the production of some of the worst evils of the last century. If such prejudice is an antipathy based upon "a faulty and inflexible generalization," as Gordon W. Alport, professor of psychology at Harvard, put it in his great work *The Nature of Prejudice*, then some of the worst massacres of that century of massacre were motivated, or at least made possible, by it. The fact that a massacre might take place in specific historical circumstances that lent a superficial plausibility to the motivating prejudice is beside the point. That Rwanda was being invaded by Tutsi rebels, and in Burundi to the south a massacre by a Tutsi government of every single Hutu who had attended secondary school had taken place within living memory, does not serve to excuse a genocide that could have taken place only upon a foundation of long-standing prejudice. One might put it like this: no prejudice, no genocide.

Even the entirely laudable desire to avoid future genocide, however, does not permit us to commit errors of logic. If the existence of widespread prejudice is necessary for the commission of genocide, it is certainly not a sufficient one. Nor does it follow from the fact that all who commit genocide are prejudiced that all who are prejudiced commit genocide. It is certainly true that if prejudice were a necessary condition of genocide, then to cure mankind of prejudice would cure it also of genocide; but what is desirable, at least in this one respect, is not necessarily possible. And an unachievable goal cannot be a desirable one.

I very much doubt whether anyone, at least in polite company, would admit to a prejudice about anything. To admit to a prejudice is to proclaim oneself a bigot, the kind of person who can't, or worse still won't, examine his pre-conceptions and opinions, and is, as a consequence, narrow in his sympathies, pharisaic in his judgments, xenophobic in his attitudes, rigid in his principles, punitive towards his inferiors, obsequious to his superiors, and convinced of his own rectitude. Such a one is not very attractive, to say the least. Better, then, to swallow one's prejudices than admit them in public.

To judge by self-report, we have never lived in such un-prejudiced times, with so many people in complete control of their own opinions, which are, as a result, wholly sane, rational, and benevolent. Nobody judges anything, any person or any question, except by the light of the evidence and his own reason. Of course, not quite everyone in the world has yet reached this state of enlightenment: *The Protocols of the Learned Elders of Zion* are still to be found in the book-stores of the Middle East, bizarre cults flourish in the midst of the most technologically advanced societies, and ancient hatreds flourish in remote, and not so remote, corners of the world. Blacks cannot safely walk the streets of Moscow, it is better not to be a Hindu in Pakistan or Bangladesh, and so on and so forth; but in the intellectual heartlands of the world, where we all happen to live, prejudice has relaxed its iron grip upon our minds and reason now rules.

An unprejudiced person is the opposite of the preju-diced one. He subjects all his presuppositions (and other thoughts) to constant re-examination; he is broad in his sympathies; hesitant and generous in his judgments; is a citizen of the world rather than of any particular part of it; subtle and flexible in his conceptions; more inclined to understand than to condemn; and, despite a certain self-satisfaction, which is the natural consequence of an awareness of his own passionless virtue, is conscious of his own limitations. He knows, as Dr. Chasuble in *The Importance of Being Earnest* knew, that he is susceptible to draughts.

The man without prejudices, or rather, the man who declares himself such, is a man who is terrified to be thought first bigoted, and second, so weak of mind, so lacking in individuality and mental power, that he cannot think for himself. For his opinions, he has to fall back on the shards of wisdom, or more likely unwisdom, which constitute prejudice. Every proper man, then, is a Descartes on every subject and every question that comes before him. In other words, he seeks that indubitable Cartesian point from which, and from which only, it is possible to erect a reasonable opinion—that is to say, an opinion that is truly his own and owes nothing to unexamined pre-suppositions. The answer to every question, therefore, has to be founded on first principles that are beyond doubt, or else it is shot through with prejudice. Whether the person who declares himself free of prejudice knows it or not, whether or not he has ever read the *Discourse on Method*, he is a belated Cartesian:

> I decided to feign that everything that had entered
> my mind hitherto was no more than the illusions of
> dreams. But immediately upon this I noticed that

while I was trying to think everything false, it must needs be that I, who was thinking this, was something. And observing that this truth "I think, therefore I exist" was so solid and sure that the most extravagant suppositions of skeptics could not overthrow it, I judged that I need not scruple to accept it as the first principle of philosophy that I was seeking.

2 | The Uses of Metaphysical Skepticism

WE MAY INQUIRE why it is that there are now so many Descartes in the world, when in the seventeenth century there was only one. Descartes, be it remembered, who so urgently desired an indubitable first philosophical principle, was a genius: a mathematician, physicist, and philosopher who wrote in prose of such clarity, that it is still the standard by which the writing of French intellectuals is, or ought to be, judged. Have we, then, bred up a race of philosophical giants, whose passion is to examine the metaphysics of human existence? I hope I will not be accused of being an Enemy of the People when I beg leave to doubt it.

The popularity of the Cartesian method is not the consequence of a desire to remove metaphysical doubt, and find certainty, but precisely the opposite: to cast doubt on everything, and thereby increase the scope of personal license, by destroying in advance any philosophical basis for the limitation of our own appetites. The radical skeptic, nowadays at least, is in search not so much of truth, as of liberty—that is to say, of liberty conceived of the largest field imaginable for the satisfaction of his whims. He is in the realm of moral conceptions what the man who refuses to marry is in the realm of relationships: he is reluctant to foreclose on any possibilities by imposing limits on himself, even ones that are taken to be purely symbolic. I once had a patient who attempted suicide because her long-time lover refused to propose to her. I asked him the reason for his refusal, and he replied that it (marriage) was only a piece of paper and meant nothing. "If it is only a piece of paper and means nothing," I asked him, "why do you not sign it? According to you, it would change nothing, but it would give her a lot of pleasure." Suddenly, becoming a man of the deepest principle, he said that he did not want to live a charade. I could almost hear the argument that persuaded the man that he was right: that true love and real commitment are affairs of the heart, and need no sanction of the church or state to seal them.

The skepticism of radical skeptics who demand a Cartesian point from which to examine any question, at least any question that has some bearing on the way they ought to conduct themselves, varies according to subject matter. Very few are so skeptical that they doubt that the sun will rise tomorrow, even though they might have difficulty offering evidence for the heliocentric (or any other) theory of the solar system. These skeptics believe that when they turn the light switch, the light will come on, even though their grasp of the theory of electricity might not be strong. A ferocious and insatiable spirit of inquiry overtakes them, however, the moment they perceive that their interests are at stake—their interests here being their freedom, or license, to act upon their whims. Then all the resources of philosophy are available to them in a flash, and are used to undermine the moral authority of custom, law, and the wisdom of ages.

3 | History Teaches Us Anything We Like

THE SLIGHTEST ACQUAINTANCE with history should be more than sufficient to persuade anyone that custom, law, and the wisdom of ages have often been oppressive and worse than oppressive. There is nothing quite so easy to abuse as authority, and the inclination to do so is present, if not in all, then in most human hearts. That is precisely why we do not trust dictators even when—or especially if—they achieved power by rebellion against another established dictatorial order. If it hadn't been for the photograph taken by the Cuban photographer Alberto Korda, Ernesto Guevara would have been recognized by now as the arrogant, adolescent, power-hungry egotist that he undoubtedly was.

A certain historiography persuades us that the wisdom of the past is always an illusion, and that the history of authority is nothing but the history of its abuse. It is not difficult to construct such a history, of course, for there is a lamentable surfeit of evidence in its favor. In a recent book entitled *Menace in Europe*, for example, the talented American journalist Claire Berlinski tells us that war and genocide are not part of the history of Europe, but constitute the whole of its history. She arrives at this conclusion by looking at European history through the lens of the Holocaust and a list of wars that fills an entire page of print. (Was it not the great Gibbon himself who said, without his accustomed irony, that history was but the record of the follies and crimes of mankind?) Miss Berlinski's is an example of what might be called the nothing-but school of historiography, by means of which a narrative is constricted from highly selected facts in order to verify a key to the understanding of everything. (Here is a baleful example of the operation of a preconceived idea.) A present discontent is read backwards, or traced by a golden thread, through the whole of history, and made to supply that history with an immanent meaning and teleology.

The golden thread could just as easily be that of something positive as negative, of course. In his great history of England, Macaulay wrote:

the history of our country during the last hundred and sixty years is eminently the history of physical, moral and intellectual improvement. And this is the way the history of medicine, for example, used to be written, principally by doctors in their retirement, as a form of ancestor-worship (no doubt in the hope that they, too, would become ancestors worthy of worship). In this version, the history of medicine was that of the smooth and triumphant ascent of knowledge and technique, to our current state of unprecedented enlightenment. But then the social historians gained control of the field, and the history of medicine became that of a self-perpetuating male elite whose main interest was in increasing its social status and income, since it is clear that for centuries it possessed no knowledge or skill that could have helped its patients, rather the reverse, and that distinguished it, in point of effectiveness, from the quacks against whom it relentlessly and ruthlessly struggled, but whom it occasionally co-opted.

If the Whig interpretation of history is plausible or applicable anywhere, it is in the history of medicine. The fact of progress, as Macaulay called it, is scarcely deniable: no one, I think, would choose pre-anesthetic, pre-aseptic methods of surgery—to take but one obvious example—for himself. Moreover, the alternative historiography of medicine would have to account for that progress: how was it that an unscrupulous group of men, concerned mainly for their status and income, did, as a matter of fact, bring about such dramatic progress? Since the fact adduced by the social historians in advance of their historiography genuinely *are* facts, and not artifacts, and likewise the facts adduced by the Whig historians of medicine, the best way to resolve the discrepancy between the two schools is by reference to Ranke's famous remark—often taken as absurdly naïve from the philosophical point of view—that history is what happened, which is to say *all* of what happened. But a map of the world that reproduced all the details of the world, in the same size and proportion as the world itself, would not be a map of the world, but a parallel model or reproduction of the world. Some selection is therefore always necessary which, unless it be entirely at random, thus rendering it theoretically incomprehensible and practically useless, itself requires an underlying principle, or at least broad outlook.

The Whig historians of medicine choose their facts for one purpose—if not self-glorification, then at least self-congratulation—the social historians for another, namely denigration, or at least deflation. At the very time Macaulay was writing his history, Engels was writing his *Condition of the Working Class in England*. How were such very different views of the same object possible by men of intelligence, learning, and talent?

Perhaps the answer can best be appreciated in our response to the tremendous current economic growth in India and China. Some see this only as progress: the emergence of hundreds of millions of people from poverty into the sunny uplands of consumption. Others see in it only a polluted environment and the destruction of ancient ways of life, in favor of a homogenized, inauthentic, superficial, universal lifestyle, with increasing disparities of wealth and poverty into the bargain.

Facts alone (*à la* Gradgrind) cannot compel the framework into which they are fitted, though they may encourage the more intellectually honest of us to reconsider our framework. Inconvenient facts usually spur us to heroic efforts of rationalization to preserve our outlook, rather than to honest re-examination; in medical practice I have been struck by the capacity of even intellectually ungifted people to manufacture an infinitude of rationalizations almost instantaneously in defense of a course of action upon which they have already decided, in spite of the abundant evidence that it will be disastrous. When a doctor proposes an eminently sensible course of action to a patient, based upon the most compelling evidence, and the patient replies, "Yes, but...," the doctor might as well give up there and then, for however many rejoinders he may make to the patient's irrational objections, he will never prevail by reaching the end of the infinite regress. Of course, such stubbornness is not at the root only of much human folly; it is at the root of much, perhaps most, human wisdom, too.

4 | Why We Prefer the History of Disaster to that of Achievement

IT IS HARDLY a matter of dispute that the Whig interpretation of history is not much in favor nowadays, even in the sphere in which it is most plausible, and at least as plausible as any other interpretation. The crime-and-folly view is much preferred. Miss Berlinski confines her historiography to European history, in order to contrast it with American history, but it would not be so very difficult to construct an American history along similar lines. From the historiographic point of view, the expansion of European settlement was nothing but the despoliation of the original inhabitants and owners of the land; the War of Independence was sparked by an awareness of the long-term significance of Lord Mansfield's ruling that a slave was free as soon as he reached British soil, which meant that slavery had no long-term future under British rule; and the continuing and unabated travails of blacks in America establish beyond all reasonable doubt the hypocritical nature of the founding philosophy, which is just a cloak for economic and racial privilege. As for Asia and Africa, the task of writing a history that is the mirror-image of the Whig interpretation would be not difficult at all.

But perhaps the most startling example of the crime-and-folly school of historiography is that of Australia. This vast country is so endowed with everything that the population of a country could reasonably want that it is often called by its own inhabitants *the Lucky Country*. Actually, luck has little to do with it; no one refers to Argentina, similarly endowed, as a lucky country. But a country whose problems, by comparison with those of all other countries, are minor, and disproportionately caused by the inherent and inescapable difficulties of human existence (or Original Sin, if you prefer), rather than by defective political arrangements, does not necessarily please the intellectuals, who are left with nothing, or nothing very much, to think about and rectify.

It was therefore a godsend—to Australian intellectuals, that is—when it was discovered, or rather asserted, that the country was founded upon the worst of all possible acts, namely genocide. Here, at last, was something for Australian intellectuals really to get their teeth into. The Tasmanian aborigines died out about sixty years after the settlement of the island by the British, and the historians claimed that this was the result not of accident, but of deliberate policy. Present-day Australians, therefore, are little better than very rich men whose fortunes were founded upon a great crime, which Balzac considered to be typical of the whole class of rich men. Australians are leading their happy and prosperous lives on a foundation of corpses; penitential angst is therefore in order.

The Tasmanian genocide was soon accepted worldwide as an indisputable fact. Indeed, whenever a journalist anywhere needs a list of genocides, the Tasmanian rarely fails to appear in it. When, therefore, the Australian historian, Keith Windschuttle, published an enormous and very detailed book examining the evidence for the genocide, and found such evidence had been misconstrued where it had not been entirely fabricated, you might have supposed the world in general, and Australia in particular, would have breathed a sigh of relief: here was one genocide the less with which to upbraid humanity. But you would have been mistaken. Screams of pain rent the air and the author was reviled. Irrespective of the historical truth of the matter (and as far as I am aware, Mr. Windschuttle's most serious claims have not been refuted), it was clear that a sector of, if not the entire, Australian intelligentsia actually *wanted* there to have been a genocide. Why?

I pass over in silence the fact that the great Australian Original Sin might lend power and importance to the intellectual episcopacy (ably assisted by its attendant bureaucracy) of the Church of Verbal Atonement. The love of truth, while it exists, is generally weaker than the love of power. Rather, I refer to the psychological effects and moral consequences of the crime-and-folly version of history, so amply justified by the Tasmanian genocide.

If history is indeed but the record of extreme nastiness, then we have nothing to learn from it except that we, who of course are people of unalloyed good will, must do things—everything—differently in the future. The moral reflections of people in the past were nothing but a fig leaf for their own misbehavior on a grand scale—sheer hypocrisy, in fact. In the words of Doctor Johnson, they discoursed like angels but behaved like men, and they honored every one of their precepts more in the breach than in the observance. In the absence of any religious conception of Original Sin (by comparison with an historical conception of a foundational injustice, such as the Tasmanian genocide), by means of which the imperfectability of man could be accepted, without at the same time absolving him of the need individually to strive for virtue, either perfect moral consistency or complete amoralism becomes the standard of judgment. Of course, those who still believe in the religious conception of Original Sin, even as a metaphor, are now very few, at least among the class of people who set the intellectual and moral tone of society as a whole.

Whether amoralism or moral perfectionism is chosen as the standard, one great advantage accrues: it frees us from the weight of the past. Free of any inherited taint, we have not only the right, but the duty to work everything out for ourselves, without reference to what anyone else has ever thought. We are moral atoms in motion through a vacuum, to whom the past means nothing, or at least nothing positive or worthy of emulation, or even maintenance. It is rather something to be avoided at all cost, lest it infects one with its crimes and follies.

5 | The Effect of Pedagogy Without Prejudice

IF ONE IS morally obliged to clear one's mind of the detritus of the past, in order to become a fully autonomous moral agent, it would seem to follow that we have an obligation not to fill the minds of the young with any detritus of our own manufacture. It is hardly surprising, then, that we increasingly invest children with authority over their own lives, and at ever earlier ages. Who are we to tell them what to do? The word "pupil" has almost been eliminated from usage in the English language, and has been replaced with "student." The two words have very different connotations. A pupil is under the tutelage or direction of someone who knows what the pupil, for his own good, ought to know and to learn; a student has matured to the point at which his own curiosity or ambition permit him to follow his own inclinations, at least to some extent, where his studies are concerned. Of course, there is, and ought to be, no sharp dividing line between these two phases of an educational career, any more than there is between infancy and childhood, childhood and adolescence, and adolescence and adulthood. The absence of clear demarcations, however, does not mean that there is no difference between infancy and adulthood. No doubt the length of the phases of an educational career ought to vary according to the characteristics of the person involved. Perhaps some children are so naturally curious, and with such an instinct for the important and useful, that they can be left unguided almost from the first. But unflattering as it may be for our conception of human nature, this cannot be true of most children, who are not self-propelling along the paths of knowledge and wisdom.

Not all attempts to guide children on to these paths are successful, needless to say, as the disorder that prevails in so many of our schools amply testifies. But this in turn is evidence of a failure by parents to inculcate self-control in their offspring. And this is the result of investing their children with an authority to make choices and exercise vetoes as soon as they are able to express, or even to indicate them.

An interesting, if unintended, illustration of this appeared in a recent edition of the most prestigious general medical journal in the world, *The New England Journal of Medicine*. An editorial considered the relation between the epidemic of childhood obesity that is afflicting America and the rest of the Western world (and, indeed, the affluent classes of the rest of the world), and the advertising for fatty, salty junk food directed at children. The editorial, in my view unexceptionally, came to the conclusion that such advertising should not be permitted. It did not, however, mention the underlying premise that made such advertising immoral: namely, that it aimed deliberately at children who were not yet sufficiently old or autonomous to assess its claims or resist its charms.

It is difficult to know in advance what practical effect a ban on advertising junk food to children might have (I suspect it would be slight), but the editorial was very revealing of what, for lack of a better term, I shall call the Zeitgeist.

For the editorial stated that the advertisements gave children the impression that the junk foods in question were made just for them, and that they as children knew best what was good for them, and should therefore be the arbiters of what they ate. And this, said the editorial, made it more difficult for parents to control their children's diet.

Not a word was said about parents' proper authority over their own children. (We are speaking here of children of a very young age. According to the evidence, the obesity of children begins very early in their lives, well before anything that could possibly be construed as the age of reason. The pattern of overindulgence, principally in what is bad for them, is established before they go to school.) The author of the editorial regarded the television on which advertisements for junk food currently appear as a natural phenomenon, like the atmosphere, over the watching and influence of which parents could be expected to exercise no control. But what kind of parents, one might ask, is incapable of saying No when children want something they should not have?

Lazy or sentimental parents, no doubt. They use junk food in much the same way as (though with far less excuse than) Victorian parents used Godfrey's Cordial, that is to say opium in syrup, to stop the crying and screaming. But there is more to it than that. Anyone who has observed a mother in a shop or supermarket solicitously and even anxiously bending over a three- or four year-old child to ask him what he would like for his next meal will understand the sovereignty over choice that is now granted to those who have neither experience nor powers of discrimination enough to exercise it on the basis of anything other than the merest whim, without regard to the consequences. By abdicating their responsibility in this fashion, in the name of not passing on their own prejudices or preconceptions to their children, and not imposing their own view of what is right upon them, they enclose their children within the circle of their childish tastes. In the name of the struggle against prejudice and illegitimate authority, they instill a culinary prejudice that, though self-evidently harmful, is far more restrictive in the long run than any they might have instilled by the firm exercise of their authority; for, in the absence of experience, children will always choose the same thing, the thing that is most immediately attractive or gratifying to them.

The precocity encouraged by too-early an assumption of the responsibility for making a choice, as if children were the customers of their parents rather their offspring, is soon followed by arrested development. A young child, constantly consulted over his likes and dislikes, learns that life is, and ought to be, ruled by his likes and dislikes. He is not free of prejudices just because he is free of his parents' prejudices. On the contrary, he is a slave to his own prejudices. Unfortunately, they are harmful both to him as an individual, and to the society of which he is a member.

6 | Prejudice Necessary to Family Life

THERE USED TO BE a prejudice, almost throughout society, that families should sit down together to eat around a table. It was a ritual that was entirely normal, or perhaps I should say second-nature, to them. (Habit is behavioral prejudice.) I doubt whether more than one in a hundred such families could have provided anything like a coherent argument for conducting their meals as they did, or oppose counter-arguments to anyone who might argue the contrary. It is doubtful whether they ever thought about it; they did what they did because it was what people like themselves did.

This unthinking ritual, however, has eroded rapidly under the assault of rationalist criticism, to the point where children in more than a third of British households never eat meals at a table with other members of their family. Indeed, the possibility of doing so does not arise, since there is no longer a dining table in the household. In my experience as a doctor visiting households in less favored urban areas, I found very little evidence, not only of meals having been taken in common within them, but of cooking ever having taken place within them. The re-heating of prepared foods was the nearest many residents came to cooking. Many of the prisoners in the prison in which I worked as a doctor had never, in their entire lives, sat down to eat at a table with another human being: they did not know what it was to do so. From childhood, they had grazed when and where they felt like it, as herbivores on a savannah—though their grazing was solitary rather than in herds. The Englishman's street is now his dining room, and helps to explain why the streets are so littered, the detritus of fast food being discarded where it is solipsistically consumed.

The prejudice in favor of family meals as the means by which people should, for preference, take their sustenance, broke down because of insistent criticism. First was criticism of the family itself. For well over a century, the unhappiness of families has been an important—perhaps the most important—subject of literature. As Tolstoy justly remarked, every unhappy family is unhappy in its own way; here, then, is a theme with an infinite number of variations. (Happy families, being all happy in the same way, offer no such inexhaustible theme.) Ibsen, and even more Strindberg, gave to the family an entirely new connotation, that of domestic guerrilla warfare that ceases only with divorce or death. Who can forget the marital sniping of Strindberg's *The Dance of Death*, so convincingly portrayed that one is almost immediately convinced that all close relations between men and women must end in this fashion, or at least be disguised versions of it? And of course it is a matter of common observation that there are few fates in life, short of famine and civil war, more wretched than that of an unhappy marriage. Before the days of easy divorce, husband and wife were often chained together as if by iron. Unless they were able to console themselves elsewhere, sexually or otherwise, their lives were a living hell.

Such criticism did not fail in its effect. A prejudice in favor of family life was gradually transmuted into a prejudice against it. The cruelty and wickedness of another prejudice, which had gone hand-in-hand with that in favor of the family, was discovered: the prejudice against illegitimate children. Illegitimate children were often unjustly stigmatized—as if they could have chosen their mode of entry into the world—and the mothers treated as outcasts. A medical colleague of mine was once charged with the task of emptying an old Victorian lunatic asylum of its inmates (partly from motives of humanity, and partly from those of economy, so that property developers could transform the outwardly splendid buildings into luxury flats for the sane and upwardly mobile). My colleague discovered, in one of the back wards where the doctors seldom ventured, an inmate of nearly seventy years' residence, whose only madness had been to give birth to an illegitimate child all those years ago. Here was a life blasted by a censorious, unthinking, and cruel prejudice. A murderer, provided he was not one of the small minority to be executed, would not have been treated so harshly, and for so many years.

The horror of unhappy marriage, and the cruelty of the prejudice against illegitimate children and those who gave birth to them, became truths universally, and even joyfully, acknowledged. That they were partial truths was lost sight of by reformers; the part was taken for the whole, and a universal remedy sought so that no such evil should ever occur again. The reformers lost sight of the imperfectability of human existence; since all miseries had specific causes, misery as such must be capable of abolition, without the introduction of new evils to replace the old.

The solution, then, was to destroy the prejudice—philosophical, social, and economic—in favor of the family structure that wrought so much harm. All would be well if people were allowed to choose their own forms of close association, unbiased by any social or economic pressure to conform to any particular pattern. Affection would then be unconstrained, rather than forced, and therefore false. All responsibilities would be freely entered into, and would thus partake of real or true morality rather than mere social convention. (Not long ago, I watched an old British comedy film from the 1950s, in which a young man of the upper-middle class had made a working-class girl pregnant. The girl's indignant father demanded that the young man should marry his daughter, a demand whose justice he understood and at once agreed to. The audience howled with laughter at the primitive idea that the future birth of a child created an inescapable obligation on the part of the father. In less than half a century, the prejudice of centuries had been over-turned, made to appear ridiculous, and replaced by another, the unedifying practical consequences of which I saw daily in my work as a doctor.)

7 | One Prejudice Always Replaced by Another

TO OVERTURN A prejudice is not to destroy prejudice as such. It is rather to inculcate another prejudice. The prejudice that it is wrong to bear a child out of wedlock has been replaced by the prejudice that there is nothing wrong with it at all. Interestingly, the class that first objected on intellectual grounds to the original prejudice, namely the well-educated upper-middle class, is the least likely to behave as if that original prejudice were unjustified. In other words, for that class the matter is principally one of intellectual preening and point-scoring, of appearing bold, generous, imaginative, and independent-minded in the eyes of their peers, rather than a matter of practical policy. When George Bernard Shaw characterized marriage as a legalized form of prostitution, he was not so much demanding justice and equality for women, as he was encouraging the dissolution, even as an ideal, of permanent bonds between a man and a woman. Unfortunately, mass-bastardy is not liberating for women.

But what does this prove, you might ask? Is not the problem a hangover from the original prejudice?

A glimpse of an important aspect of the reality of mass-bastardization (at least in Britain) may be had from a report recently published by the Joseph Rowntree Trust, a British charity devoted to the study and elimination of urban poverty. The researchers interviewed forty-one teenage girls, some of them as young as thirteen, who had decided to have a baby. (The writers of the report failed to remark that most of their subjects had been, in the eyes of the law, victims of a sexual crime, an odd omission in a society hysterically obsessed by the dangers of pedophilia.)

The report quotes the girls verbatim, and the first thing that strikes the reader is their incoherence in their native, and only, language. Their vocabulary is impoverished, their syntax abominable. They struggle to make themselves understood: like the victims of certain kinds of stroke, they have not the words to articulate their feelings and thoughts. Perhaps this is not altogether surprising, for one of the things they have in common is their disdain of school and education (admittedly not the same thing, or even faintly connected, in the world in which they were brought up). The intergenerational effect is evident:

> I could of done a lot better... I don't think my mum—my [absent] dad, sort of, would say, of, yeah— yeah—I want the best for you... my mum was like, "Just go to school." She didn't really like, ask for homework and stuff—to see like, when it wasn't done. Kind of, she didn't ask me if it had been done or anything like that.

(Note the passive voice where homework is concerned. She speaks as if homework did children rather than children did homework. One may wonder whether it would not have been better for her future if the child had not grown up where there was a social prejudice in favor of education, rather than the reverse.)

The girls interviewed by the authors had a profound sense of their own social authority—a prejudice, in fact, since they derived it not from personal reflection on philosophical principles, but from unthinking acceptance of the social mores into which they were born. A fourteen-year-old girl said:

> Some teachers were OK—other teachers I used to swear at—I didn't like them at all.

The idea that dislike of someone was not sufficient grounds to swear at him, that tolerable social relations require self-control, that living with others imposed a duty of restraint, had not been inculcated in her as a prejudice, and it was now unlikely that she would ever learn it, let alone conform her behavior to it. The less than encouraging consequence was that she would continue to see all human relations as a power struggle that she was likely, on most occasions, to lose, given her relative poverty, lack of education, vulnerability and exploitability as a single mother, and utter dependence for her sustenance on a state bureaucracy for which she was but a number, with all the resultant frustration, misery, and victimization that follows from such a position.

Another girl, telling her interviewer why she did not like school, said:

> all the teachers made you stand up when they walked into the room. Why should I stand up? I don't stand

up for my [separated] parents, so why am I gonna
stand up for them? It was a—very much, you're the
child, I'm the teacher.

Contained in this passage is the assumption that, since all
people are created equal, all social relations must be conducted on the same and equal basis: that what is appropriate with one's parents (not, of course, honor or obedience)
is appropriate with everyone, in all circumstances. Authority derives from drawing breath, by the secular equivalent of
divine providence—that is to say, by natural right. Not surprisingly, it comes hard to such people that the world in
general is not as interested in them as the people in their
immediate circle are. And when this attitude of inherent
authority has entered the fabric of the presuppositions of
everyone around them, it is again not surprising that when
teachers inform parents of the misconduct of their offspring, they, the parents, take it as a personal insult and
blame not their children, who are the outer limits of their
own egos, as they would once have done, but the teachers
and the school, who have committed the crime of *lèse-
majesté*. A blind prejudice in favor of constituted authority
has been replaced by a blind prejudice that authority, other
than one's own, is inherently illegitimate.

No one would suggest that parents ought to have
unyielding faith in teachers that is impervious to evidence
of individual malignity; but a prejudice that, when teachers
complain of the conduct of a child, they are more likely to
be in the right than in the wrong, would conduce overall to
the improvement, rather than to the deterioration, of a
child's conduct.

We can rid ourselves of any particular attitude to any given question, no doubt, but we cannot give up having any attitude whatsoever towards it.

8 | The Cruel Effect of Not Instilling the Right Prejudices

THE GIRLS INTERVIEWED in the previously discussed report were in many ways in an unenviable, indeed pitiable, situation. For the most part, they came from precisely the kind of homes that they were so obviously in the process of reproducing:

> I do not know who he is [said one of the girls of her father]—I know his name and I know where he's living, but I—I don't know what to believe. I don't know whether—I don't know whether to go and find him or just leave it the way it is, because it is true, what my mum was saying—about my dad leaving me—then it would be off if I didn't know him. . .

Emerging from a loveless environment—in which hostility, not just to people, but to the world in general, is always more marked than tenderness—the girls seek to assuage their need for love by bringing into the world a being upon whom they can lavish that unsatisfied emotion that dwells in their heart. They hope the child will reciprocate their love unconditionally, like a soft toy or—at the limit of their imaginative capacity—a dog. A thirteen year-old with a baby said:

I—I had a really, really bad childhood—I just—'cos my parents aren't very good parents so—and (um) I—I just thought a baby would give me that stability and also give me something that would love me unconditionally—you know—never thought it would leave me and—'cos it'd be mine—nobody could take it away or—and it would be mine. . .

Another girl, a few years older, said:

Maybe it's just—yeah, because maybe just—might be (um)—it just feels great when—when like, you've got a child who just—you know—following you around, telling you they love you and I think that's—it is quite selfish, but that's one of the reasons why I became a mum because I wanted someone who'll—you know— love 'em to bits 'cos it's not just your child who's the centre of your world—the parents are the centre of the child's world, and that feels great, so I think— yeah—yeah, that's—that's—it's brilliant.

As we can see in these sad, sub-Cartesian, but nonetheless revealing comments, there is not much in the way of moral reflection here (apart from brief acknowledgment of possible selfishness, outweighed, of course, by the brilliance of having an animated cuddly toy all to oneself that, it may safely be predicted, will turn difficult soon after it can walk and talk, prompting the desire for another such cuddly toy, and explaining the fact that in Britain, at least, a quarter of all children born to girls under the age of eighteen are second children). And this is hardly the girl's own fault: no sensible person would expect adolescents of thirteen or fifteen, even those growing up in homes in which abstract and intellectual discussions are frequent and sophisticated, to be able to plot a reasonable, sensible, constructive, or fruitful path for themselves without guidance, occasional prodigies of precocious wisdom notwithstanding. They need first to be inculcated with useful prejudices before they can be expected to make for themselves the most fundamental (and difficult) choices in life. Is it right—is it kind or decent, let alone realistic or sensible—to expect a girl who describes in the following fashion her decision to have a child to generate moral principles for herself?

> 'Cos I wanted children—and I wasn't—you know—
> doing anything else really—I wasn't working and—so
> it wasn't—nothing just—nothing getting in the way
> really—so—I was, like lost—I didn't know what to do
> with myself, 'cos I was just working and thinking, this
> is pointless—I'm not enjoying this, or I'm not enjoy-
> ing what I'm doing at the moment.

Would it not have been better, for her in particular and for the world in general, if she had been instilled at an early age with a prejudice that she should not have a child until such time as she was able, with the child's father, to offer the child a stable base from which he or she would later be able to launch his or her own life?

By the time she comes to this conclusion herself (and from talking to such girls, I have discovered that it is likely that she will do so), it will be too late.

9 | The Inevitability of Prejudice

OF COURSE, it does not follow from the fact that the girls (and presumably the boys with whom they consort) do not share the prejudice against illegitimate childbirth that they have no prejudice on the subject at all. Prejudice is like Nature in the famous line from the Epistles of Horace: you may toss her out with a pitchfork, yet she will soon return.

Thus the girls who at so early an age knowingly broke what would once have been a taboo against childbirth out of wedlock were not so much breaking a taboo, of whose very former existence they were now probably only barely aware, as acting in conformity to what they saw around them and what they thought was expected of them:

> My mum's never had a job—she just had me and my sisters—like, quite young. Like, a housewife-type thing. And that's what all my friends' mums are too. There's tons of teenage mums round here—I don't know why—nobody looks at me funny 'cos there's so many of us.

This is what one might call the Forty-million-Frenchmen-can't-be-wrong argument: that what other people do, provided they do it in sufficient numbers, is a guarantee of its rightness. We are very far here from the autonomous and inquiring individual of John Stuart Mill's somewhat limited imagination, who always reasons out for himself what he should do; and yet, if you were to tax any of these followers of the herd with the social undesirability of her conduct, she would immediately resort to first principle, or something like it, in justifying herself. Indeed, some of the girls in the herd headed off criticism in advance of its having been made (it never was). A girl of sixteen said:

> I don't care anyway [about criticism]—I'm not too young—but it's not about age, I do believe that.

In a sense, of course, she is perfectly right. The argument against unmarried teenage pregnancy is largely a statistical one: the outcome for mother and child is more than usually likely to be a bad one. Moreover, that negative outcome will impose severe costs on third parties who had nothing to do with the original decision to have the child. But the bad outcome is not absolutely inevitable, for in human affairs there is rarely a one-to-one correspondence between decisions or events and their outcome. Nor do we automatically condemn people for attempting what is statistically unlikely. Only one in ten applicants to medical school is admitted, but we do not deprecate the conduct of the unsuccessful candidates, who knew in advance that the odds were stacked against them. Indeed, all great achievement is against the odds. When a novelist sits down to write a novel, he must be aware that his chances of writing a classic that will outlast the few weeks after its publication, of joining Flaubert and Tolstoy, are infinitesimal, but we do not therefore condemn his attempt. In like fashion, the unmarried teenage mother can appeal to the fact that she is an individual and not just a member of a class of people.

You cannot deduce all the characteristics of an individual from the membership of the class to which he or she belongs, when those characteristics are variably distributed within it. For it might very well be true that the children of single teenage mothers are far more likely than other children to end up delinquent or criminal, to take drugs or drink heavily, to be illiterate and unemployable, to suffer severe psychological problems, and so forth, but it is also perfectly possible that many of them will do, be or suffer none of these things, and have an existence that is, to them at least, perfectly satisfactory. And if it is true that human life is a good, or an end, in itself, and that in a broad sense it is sacred, how can we lament the fact that the girls in the report I have cited have brought additional such life into the world? They themselves are vehemently opposed to abortion, which they believe to be little short of murder. Asked whether she had considered abortion, one girl explained that she hadn't:

> 'Cos it's a life—I don't—I don't think it's right to kill a life no matter if . . . it's just not . . . don't do it.

Another said:

> I was saying "Oh I'll have an abortion"—but I know I couldn't do it. . . I don't agree with it at all. It's just wrong and I'll never do it to a baby.

Nor would the girls be at the end of their philosophical resources if taxed about the foolishness or immorality of

35

their conduct. They might be prepared to concede the increased statistical likelihood of their offspring suffering multiple disadvantages at all stages of life, but they would place the blame for it elsewhere, on society as a whole. They would blame the insufficient social assistance that they received, or the residual prejudice in the higher social classes against such children; they might (with some justice) point to the very poor schools their children would attend, which would fail to provide them with even the basic education that is the requisite of further personal development. In short, their decision to have a baby at a very early age without any support from the father has the consequences it does have, statistically speaking, only because of the failures of society as a whole. There is nothing wrong with the decision itself.

Moral and intellectual support for such a view, or something very like it, is not difficult to find. For example, the report quotes an article by a well-known British journalist for the liberal newspaper *The Guardian*. The journalist, Madeleine Bunting, makes much of the supposedly unalterable fact that the alternatives in life for the girls in question are not very inviting, certainly for minds filled with images of life derived from glossy celebrity magazines and television dramas:

> So when a girl at 17 decides to go ahead and have a baby, there is no tragedy of lost opportunity other than the local checkout till waiting for her low-paid labour ... these teen mums are making reasonable—even moral—decisions about what they value in life, and what they want to do with their lives. ... How did

opting for a baby and motherhood over shelf-stacking
ever become a tragedy?

Although the writer of these words would probably pride
herself on her broadmindedness, her lack of common prejudice, there are nevertheless several non-trivial assump-
tions in the passage that betray, or are themselves, profound
prejudices. First is the assumption that there is something
wrong, humiliating, even dishonorable about low-paid,
unskilled labor (though by low-paid in the modern context,
be it remembered, we do not mean starvation wages). I am no
economist, but the demand that cheap labor become expensive labor without any improvement in its quality or output,
in order to gratify the natural desire of the unskilled for a
higher standard of living, or at any rate level of consumption,
irrespective of its effect on the rest of the economy, does not
seem to me to be a recipe for long-term prosperity.

Second is the evident disdain for supermarket shelf-
stacking as an activity. Does the author, I wonder, never
shop in a supermarket? Would she prefer that supermarket
shelves remained unstacked and all the goods piled in a great
heap, for shoppers to clamber over as rubbish tips in the
Third World are clambered over by the very poor, seeking
what is valuable or desirable among the dross? It is true, of
course, that stacking supermarket shelves is not the most
intellectually demanding of jobs, but it is perfectly respectable, honest, and socially useful. So long as supermarket
shelves must be stacked—until they disappear from the face
of the earth or can be stacked in a fully automated way—
there must be supermarket shelf-stackers. Snobbish disdain
for such menial but productive activities could scarcely be

more clearly implied than by the writer above; and it is precisely this disdain, rather than anything intrinsic in the task, that renders it humiliating.

And finally, the author makes clear also that, in her opinion, once a person is a supermarket shelf-stacker, he or she is always a supermarket shelf-stacker. It is like the mark of Cain, ineradicable. This is not so, either in theory or in practice. The writer, it appears, wishes to replace a prejudice against thirteen-year-old mothers with a prejudice against eighteen-year-old supermarket shelf-stackers.

10 | The Conventionality of Unconventionality

SOME PEOPLE WISH to escape convention as others wish to escape the necessity to earn a living. Indeed, unconventionality has become for them a virtue in itself, as originality now is for people whose artistic aspirations exceed their talents. A reviewer of a biography of the late philosopher A. J. Ayer wrote in the *Times Literary Supplement*, not exactly an organ of youth counter-culture, that among Ayer's virtues was that he was unconventional. The writer did not think it was necessary to indicate in what respect—what opinion, what conduct—he was unconventional. The virtue spoke for itself, as it were.

Of course, roasting babies for breakfast is unconventional, as was (at one time) drawing attention to the iniquity of Soviet communism or racial segregation in South Africa: but it is the *form* of unconventionality that is important, evidently, not its *content*, at least for the writer of the review, who is not untypical of many intellectuals in this regard. An artist who breaks a taboo, often said to be the last remaining one, though another is soon enough found in order to be broken (one is reminded of the repeated last performances of the Australian singer, Nellie Melba), is likely to be praised for his originality, courage, and so forth, irrespective of whether the taboo ought to have been broken, or of the social effect of having done so. The habitual breakers of boundaries are not so much objecting to any particular boundary, as objecting to the existence of boundaries as such. They want a life without boundaries: civilization always has its discontents.

In a sense, every human being is original, and that without effort or self-consciousness: many of every person's utterances have never been uttered before and will never be uttered again. But the kind of originality that everyone shares is not the kind of originality that modern romantics require in order to feel fully individuated in mass society. What they need is original originality, or meta-originality, as it were. This sets up the equivalent of an arms race, with more and more extravagant gestures required to mark a person from the herd (is this necessity not a key to understanding much of the history of art in the late twentieth century?). Unfortunately, the desire to escape from convention is itself a convention. The mass bohemianization of society has not necessarily resulted in the flowering of worthwhile individuality or cultural achievement: one has only to reflect upon the small population size of medieval and renaissance Florence or Siena to realize this. One convention has been replaced by another. When I attended a bourgeois bohemian funeral in Paris recently, it was I who stood out in my dark suit and tie—so provincial, so conventional! Everyone else looked as if he or she had just popped into the cemetery after a bit of shopping in the local grocery, during a brief abandonment by the muses.

Did it matter? After all, the man principally concerned was dead and past caring, unless you believe in a surviving spirit that hovers over funerals, observing who are the true mourners and who not (some such idea is in the minds of many youthful would-be suicides). It is not difficult to construct the bohemian argument against any kind of formality of dress at funerals: that what counts is what people genuinely and authentically feel for and about the dear departed, not how they dress; that the assumption of special clothing encourages hypocrisy and pretense, as if hypocrisy and pretense were so easily eliminated from the human repertoire. For myself, I can say only that I prefer a slightly more ceremonious approach to a man's death, some visible sign that his funeral is not just one more event in the day's busy schedule, an interlude between a visit to the bank and coffee with friends, or between buying some shoes and writing an article. Whatever my preferences, however, the fact is that what started out as the rejection of convention has itself become the convention, and the adolescents who attended the funeral in their barely gentrified version of American ghetto costume will have formed the prejudice that funerals are no different, sartorially, from other gatherings, and it will not occur to them that things could be, and have been, different. If ever they were to attend a more traditional funeral, they would find it anthropologically strange, like the war-dance of South Sea natives.

Let me point out, in passing, that dressing for funerals requires an effort, which coming as you are does not.

11 | The Overestimation of Rationality in Choice

ONE OF THE sources of the prejudice against prejudice is John Stuart Mill's great tract, *On Liberty*, published in 1851. As is well known, Mill had a peculiar childhood under the tutelage of his rationalist father, who believed that right action could be reduced to an almost mathematical formula—namely, that the right act was that which produced the greatest happiness for the greatest number. The hope of Mill *senior* was that Mill *junior* would duly grow into that hitherto elusive beast, the wholly rational man, a kind of calculating machine on legs.

All went well until Mill *junior* reached the age of twenty, when he experienced a mental crisis, commonly called a nervous breakdown. Under the influence of Romantic poets such as Wordsworth and Coleridge, he realized that the somewhat desiccated notion of human existence espoused and ruthlessly pursued by his father was not adequate to meet all human needs. He was like the dutiful child of parents who belong to a rigid and exclusive religious sect, the child who discovers in his adolescence or early adulthood that his parents' beliefs, hitherto taken for granted, are without foundation and even slightly mad.

Mill resolved the problem, at least for himself, by combining the romantic cult of the individual with the puritanical utilitarianism of his father. And so powerful was this solution, at least rhetorically, that it has been adopted by much of the Western intelligentsia ever since, and through them by entire populations, whether they know it or not. All Western philosophy, the idealist philosopher of the early twentieth century, A. N. Whitehead, famously remarked, is "footnotes to Plato"; all Western social policy is footnotes to Mill, albeit with consequences of which he would not in the slightest have approved.

The desire to reconcile the irreconcilable, to render radical individualism the most social of creeds and utilitarianism the most individualistic, Mill was led to an unrealistic view of both human beings and the society in which they lived. He was inclined to suppose, as many thinkers are, that most people either were or could become, with sufficient education, like himself. In a way this does him honor, for he modestly supposed also that his own gifts were neither great nor exceptional, but this led him to imagine what is not very probable, that there would come a time when most people would be as deeply concerned with the moral foundations of human conduct as he. This in turn suggests that his knowledge of human beings in walks of life different from his own was not very extensive. This is hardly surprising, since by the time Mill came to write *On Liberty*, he and his wife led a reclusive existence.

At any rate, Mill generally overestimated the role that reasoning did, or very well could, play in normal, day-to-day life. Near the very beginning of the tract, written in such vigorous and persuasive prose that one is swept along by it, Mill inveighs against social prejudice, which he sees as a danger greater in present circumstances than openly tyrannical government:

43

> Protection, therefore, against the tyranny of the magistrate is not enough; there needs protection also against the tyranny of prevailing opinion and feeling, against the tendency of society to impose, by other means than civil penalties, its own ideas and practices as rules of conduct. . .

The individual must therefore decide for himself whether to conform to the ideas and practices of society, and this for a number of reasons. The most important of these is that the truth of any subject, no more in the empirical than in the moral realm, cannot be known once and for all, finally and indubitably, and therefore any "ideas and practices as rules of conduct" are open to question. Advance, both moral and empirical, emerges from the continual clash of opinion—this is indubitable. But even if this were not so, there is an ethical principle that would require that each man choose whether or not to conform to society's ideas and practices:

> In that part [of his conduct] which merely concerns himself, his independence is, of right, absolute. Over himself, over his own body and mind, the individual is sovereign.

Here speaks the man who is almost a recluse. It has long been an objection to Mill that, except for the anchorite in the Syrian desert who subsists on honey and locusts, no man is an island (and even an anchorite may have a mother who is disappointed by her son's choice of career); and therefore that the smallest of his acts may have some impact or consequences for others. If one amends the principle to take that part of a man's conduct that concerns principally himself, rather than only himself, one will be left with endless and insoluble disputes as to which part of his conduct that is, and the boundary separating it from the rest.

But, as the great historian Lord Acton said, "Ideas have a radiation and development, an ancestry and posterity of their own, in which men play the part of godfathers and godmothers more than that of legitimate parents." Who can doubt that many people have forgotten, for very obvious reasons, Mill's qualification of personal sovereignty, namely that it applies to conduct that "merely concerns himself?" When the person who argues for abortion on demand (and I speak as someone not totally opposed to abortion) on the grounds that a woman is the *Roi soleil* over her own body, does he not forget that the fetus is not purely of her body, but is a distinct being in formation and is, until parthenogenesis becomes the rule, the product, to use a neutral and impersonal term, of another person also? In any minimally decent world, wouldn't the father have inescapable responsibilities towards his offspring, and therefore (since there ought to be no taxation without representation), have some moral right to a say in the matter? Mill was certainly not an apologist of abortion-on-demand type egotism, either in theory, or in the example he gave to the world, but he was, in Acton's phrase, its godfather, or one of its godfathers.

While I am far from deprecating the role of intellection in human life, and sometimes even lament its absence from large parts of it, its role is inevitably far more complex than the straightforward one Mill imagined. The vast majority of men—and here I include myself, so I mean no disrespect—

cannot go through life as if it were a long series of intellectual and moral puzzles. If it were, and if we took them seriously, most of us would end up starving like Buridan's ass who, perfectly equidistant between two piles of hay, could not decide which way to turn.

12 | Authority Necessary to the Accumulation of Knowledge

ACCORDING TO MILL, no question, moral or empirical, is ever settled beyond doubt, and therefore our answers to questions moral and empirical must be forever temporary and susceptible to revision. He tells us that the truth (or perhaps we should say the truer, or the true-ish, since in his own hypothesis the truth cannot be known) emerges from a clash of opinion, false (or false-ish) and true (or true-ish). This presents him with a utilitarian argument for never suppressing opinion: if you suppress the false, you will never reach the true, and if you never reach the true, progress would be impossible.

There is a sense in which this is perfectly true, of course. A scientific milieu in which no disagreement was permitted, in which (for example) everyone was forced to agree with an official doctrine even on the smallest matters, is not one in which much advance would be made. Within the confines of its scientific establishments, upon which its military might ultimately rested, even the Soviet Union permitted intellectual freedom. But the permission of intellectual freedom, however great, does not dispose of the question of authority, even in the freest of societies. The possibilities and resources of any laboratory, be it ever so well-endowed, are always finite; someone must choose among lines of research to pursue, usually on the basis of an intuition as to which is likely to be the most scientifically profitable.

Besides, it does not follow from the fact that the freedom to express falsehoods is essential to the discovery of truth, that all falsehoods are of equal, or indeed of any, value in this search. Mill, it seems, has not sufficiently frequented the company of crackpots in saloon bars to appreciate this. The suppression of opinion, by outlawing it, that the Pacific Ocean is composed exclusively of melted brie, could hardly be expected to retard in any way the science of oceanography. What, in any case, would we answer to the person, if we answered him at all, who insisted that the Pacific was so composed? Would we protest that seas are just not like that? He would reply, "But the Pacific is." If we insisted, "But I have been to the Pacific, and it is made of seawater," he would demand, "When were you last there?" and, on learning that it was five years ago, would assert in triumph, "It's changed since then." If we then picked up the phone to ask someone living by the ocean whether the Pacific had changed recently into melted brie, we should have become as mad as our interlocutor.

Not every falsehood, therefore, is valuable in the search for truth; indeed, it would be the work of an hour to generate hundreds of falsehoods that were of no conceivable use or value, and that were not worth refuting.

Furthermore, it is very easy to exaggerate or overemphasize the provisional nature of scientific knowledge. When an eminent biologist of my acquaintance meets someone who tells him that, after all, science is only hypothesis, he replies, "But the blood does circulate." And in fact, we no more expect someone to perform an experiment proving that the blood does not circulate, than we expect a mathematician to come up with a proof that two and two do not equal four. The blood circulates, and we know that it circulates (even the most skeptical of epistemologists would not refuse to consult a cardiac surgeon on the grounds that he doubted whether there were sufficient grounds for belief in the circulation of the blood), yet not one in a hundred of us, I suspect, could demonstrate it to someone who, for some reason, were not aware of it, using the resources only of our own minds. Demonstration of the capillaries, vital to the whole argument and discovered by the Italian eighteenth-century microscopist Malpighi, might prove particularly difficult for the uninitiated, and it is well for the advancement of science that each generation does not have to make for itself all the discoveries of previous generations, on the grounds that they rest on authority, but rather can accept them more or less on that very authority.

The vast majority of our knowledge comes to us in the same way. I have known from a very early age that a battle took place at Hastings in the year 1066, but I still do not know how to prove that it did. To do so would require the training of a lifetime, and would necessarily inhibit my acquisition of knowledge in other directions, with the result, moreover, that it would merely confirm what I already knew, unless it were also my intention to carry out original research into that period of history. It is one of the great achievements of our civilization that, to an extent unequalled by any other, it has created the institutional means by which genuine knowledge may be sought and disseminated, and that it has simultaneously and continuously examined the strength of the evidence upon which that knowledge is based. The institutions work only to the degree that they are free, of course: not free of prejudice or preconceived ideas, for that is impossible, but free to examine such prejudice and preconceived ideas in the light of further evidence, and to reject or modify them as becomes intellectually necessary. Freedom, however, does not imply the uncritical exercise of it: the wise question only those things that are worth questioning.

Mill was not so foolish that he did not appreciate this. At times he sounds positively balanced and realistic:

> No one would assert that people ought never to put into their mode of life, and into the conduct of their concerns, any impress whatever of their own judgement or of their individual character. On the other hand, it would be absurd to pretend that people ought to live as if nothing whatever had been known in the world until they came into it; as if experience had as yet done nothing towards showing that one mode of existence, or of conduct, is preferable to another.

Mill is speaking here of moral knowledge, but the same would apply to knowledge of a more empirical kind.

Nevertheless, Mill acts as godfather to an idea that is not strictly his—namely, that one opinion is as good as another, even in matters of fact. One can see this in the modern use of the word "valid," a word that, in the mouth of students, must send shivers down the spine of academics of the old school, who have respect for truth as the object of inquiry. It is not arguments that are valid anymore, in the sense that they are constructed in accordance with the laws of logic and of evidence, but that opinions and even questions are.

For example, a British television interviewer named Jonathan Ross, known—indeed, employed by the BBC at a salary of $11,000,000 a year—for extreme vulgarity, asked the leader of the opposition party, David Cameron, whether as a youth he had masturbated while thinking of Mrs. Thatcher. This witless question, not surprisingly, drew some public criticism, to which he replied that he stood by his question, which he still considered "a valid one."

13 | The Supposed Equality of All Opinions, Provided They are One's Own

WHAT DID Jonathan Ross mean by this? We shall see in a moment; let us return briefly to Mill as unintended godfather to bad ideas.

There is no truth so certain, says Mill, that it cannot be controverted (except, perhaps, for this one). It is from this fact, or alleged fact, that he derives the utilitarian argument for freedom of expression, though of course other arguments for it are possible.

But Mill goes beyond this. He tells us that it is necessary for the development of a person's own personality that his opinions should not merely be handed down to him, but be his own. Indeed, a person who is formed by his society is less than fully human:

> He who lets the world, or his portion of it, choose his plan of life for him, has no need of any other faculty than the ape-like one of imitation.

The romantic cult of the original human being is expressed in the forceful prose of rationalism of which Mill was the master:

though the customs may be good and suitable to him, yet to conform to custom merely as custom does not educate or develop in him any of the distinctive qualities which are the distinctive endowment of a human being. The human faculties of perception, judgement, discriminative feeling, mental activity, and even moral preference are exercised only in making a choice. He gains no practice either in discerning or in desiring what is best. The mental and the moral, like the muscular, powers are improved only by being used. The faculties are called into no exercise by doing a thing merely because others do it, no more than by believing a thing only because others believe it. If the grounds of an opinion are not conclusive to a person's own reason, his reason cannot be strengthened, but is likely to be weakened, by his adopting it: and if the inducements to an act are not such as are consentaneous to his own feelings and character (where affection, or the rights of others, are not concerned), it is so much done towards rendering his feelings and character inert and torpid instead of active and energetic.

It is hardly surprising if people deduce, or at least infer, from this passage that the most important quality of an act or opinion is not that it should be right, or striving to be right (given the uncertainty of factual knowledge and the frailty of human reason), but that it should be the person's own. To hold opinions that are not one's own in Mill's sense, for example, by taking them from a trusted authority on the subject, is not to partake of "the qualities which are the distinctive endowment of a human being." In conjunction with the notion of the uncertainty of human knowledge, we see, in the necessity for all opinions to be one's own, the philosophical and psychological provenance of the modern notion of "validity." When the interviewer, Jonathan Ross, defended the question he had asked the politician by calling it "a valid question," he meant not that it was grammatically well formed, or that it raised a matter of public importance, but that the question was the product of his own unaided cerebration, if that is quite the word. A small thing, but his own!

Many an argument about substantive matters of fact is now brought to an end by one or several of the disputants claiming, at a point of irreconcilable difference, "Well, my opinion is just as valid as yours." No matter that one of the disputants among them may have made a special study of the question, has more evidence at his disposal and has constructed a logical framework for them, and that the persons who claim equal "validity" for their opinions on the matter have never before given a moment's thought to it and are thoroughly ignorant of all that is relevant to it. If nothing is certain, what are facts anyway? They are opinions. Thus freedom of opinion becomes equality of opinion: for what is the use of freedom without equality?

14 | Custom Supposedly Wrong Because It Is Custom

OF COURSE, I am not claiming that each person who claims that his opinion is equally valid with every other because it comes from that unimpeachable authority, himself, has actually read Mill on liberty. But ideas and opinions filter through society as a crystal of potassium permanganate dissolves in a beaker of water and eventually spreads its color throughout it. As men agglomerated in larger and larger cities, to perform ever more precise, frustrating, and routine tasks (a process that occurred at an accelerated pace in Mill's lifetime), so a fear developed among thinkers that Man himself was becoming just a machine, or rather a cog in a giant machine. Mill was far from the only writer concerned about the loss of individuality: Ruskin, Carlyle, and Marx shared his concern. But it was Mill who, at least in the modern world, has proved the most influential in the long run, especially after the demise of Marxian utopianism. His writing, too, is infused with utopianism, albeit of a low-grade and less strident form than Marx's. It was Mill who, though his powerful rhetoric, insinuated into society the notion of the unique beauty and utility of each person's opinions, at least in potential, provided only he could rid himself of the dross of received opinion. Received opinion is the enemy of mankind:

In our times, from the highest class of society to the lowest, everyone lives as under the eye of a hostile and dreaded censorship. Not only in what concerns others, but in what concerns themselves, the individual or the family do not ask themselves, what do I prefer? or, what would suit my character and disposition? or what would allow the best and highest in me to have fair play and enable it to grow and thrive? They ask themselves, what is suitable to my position? what is usually usually done by persons of my station and pecuniary circumstances? or (worse still) what is usually done by a person of a station and circumstances superior to mine?

The results are horrible and dehumanizing (how many intellectuals have found reasons for concluding that ninety-nine percent of their fellow-men are not really human at all?):

conformity is the first thing thought of; they like in crowds; they exercise choice only among things commonly done; peculiarity of taste, eccentricity of conduct are shunned equally with crime, until by dint of not following their nature they have no nature to follow. . .

What is the alternative to this hellish vision of men as glorified hymenopterans? Mill achieves the impossible, and reconciles the doctrines of Jean-Jacques Rousseau and Jeremy Bentham:

It is not by wearing down into uniformity all that is individual in themselves, but by cultivating it and calling it forth, that human beings become a noble and beautiful object of contemplation; and as the works partake of the character of those who do them, by the same process human life also becomes rich, diverse and animating, finishing more abundant aliment to high thoughts and elevating feelings, and strengthening the tie which binds every individual to the race, and makes the race infinitely better worth belonging to. In proportion to the development of his individuality, each person becomes more valuable to himself, and is, therefore, capable of being more valuable to others.

To which one can only reply, Oh, yeah?

For Mill, custom is an evil that is the principle obstruction to progress and moral improvement, and its grip on society is so strong that originality, unconventionality, and rebellion against it are goods in themselves, irrespective of their actual content. The man who flouts a convention *ipso facto* raises society from its torpor and lets everyone know that there are different, and better, ways of doing things. The more such people there are, the greater the likelihood of progress.

Mill lived in an optimistic age. The worst social eventuality of which he could conceive was stagnation, that is to say, a lack of progress that would otherwise have been possible. Of radical evil, in which the following century was to abound, he has nothing to say, and therefore he had no idea that a mania for progress could result in its very antithesis, or that some defense against such radical evil, of which the commission was not possible without the co-operation and participation of many men, was necessary. The abandonment of customary restraint and inverted moral prejudice was not necessarily followed by improvement.

Mill does not mention custom without hurling a brickbat at it:

> It does not occur to [anyone] to have any inclination except for what is customary. Thus the mind is bowed to the yoke. . . . The despotism of custom is everywhere the standing hindrance to human achievement, being an unceasing antagonism to the disposition to aim at something better than customary. . . . The progressive principle . . . is antagonistic to the sway of custom, involving at least emancipation from that yoke; and the contest between the two constitutes the chief interest in the history of mankind. The greater part of the world has, properly speaking, no history, because the despotism of custom is complete.

It is not very surprising if people concluded from this that a custom was not to be flouted or overthrown because of its particular content, but simply because it was a custom, and therefore deleterious—*ex officio*, as it were. This conclusion would have been much strengthened by Mill's encomium to originality, to the efforts of a man merely to be different, in order, that is, not to be better than other men are, but to distinguish himself from them:

In our time, the mere example of non-conformity, or refusal to bend the knee to custom, is deemed a service to humanity. Precisely because the tyranny of opinion is such as to make eccentricity a reproach, it is desirable, in order to break through that tyranny, that people should be eccentric.

Here, truly, is a prejudice against prejudice.

15 | A Partial Reading of Mill Leads to Unbridled Egotism

WHAT MILL APPEARS to be recommending, and what certainly he has been taken to have recommended, is that each person should set sail upon the sea of life unguided by anything other than the rudder of his own reasoning. In fact, Mill had a pretty poor opinion of most of mankind's powers in that regard, speaking disparagingly even of ninety-nine percent of educated men, let alone the rest. If the vast majority of a tiny minority couldn't think for themselves, what hope was there for the rest of humanity? There is no need to despair, however: "The honour and glory of the average man is that he is capable of following [the] initiative of all wise or noble things that come and must come from individuals." In other words, it was an excellent thing for average Germans to give up their prejudice against creating disorder on the street, attacking individuals, and smashing property, in order to follow that lonely, eccentric, and undoubtedly original man, Adolf Hitler.

That Mill was in some respects an Old Testament moralist tends to be forgotten by those who wish to see his book as a mere license for license. In fact, he disapproved as strongly as any evangelical preacher of unbridled sensuality, sexual incontinence, and so forth. He speaks disdainfully of "he who cannot restrain himself from hurtful indulgence" and of he "who pursues animal pleasures at the expense of those of feeling and intellect." He would bring no comfort to those who consider that modern family arrangements (or rather, lack of arrangements) are the natural consequence of his doctrine of liberty. "If a man," he says, "[has] undertaken the moral responsibility of a family and becomes from [intemperance or extravagance] incapable of supporting or educating them, he is deservedly reprobated and might be justly punished." Of course, someone might point out that the abandonment of responsibility for a family is not what it once was, for the state, which is, if not quite the father of the child, at least the step-father of the child, will take up the slack, and so the moral opprobrium of such abandonment is no longer justified. I doubt that Mill would have agreed; the point is, however, that people usually draw from philosophical doctrines those consequences that are in accord with their deep, or perhaps their least shallow, desires.

The idea that "the sole end for which mankind are warranted ... in interfering with the liberty of action of any of their number" is to prevent conduct that "is calculated to produce evil to someone else," in conjunction with the difficulty of deciding what an evil actually is and who is really responsible for it, while at the same time believing that diversity of conduct and moral codes is a good in itself, frees a man from complying with any custom or informal rule that has hitherto been widely respected. He is free then to conduct himself any way he wishes, as whimsically as may be, at least until someone challenges him. Conformity to any rule is felt as a wound to personal sovereignty, as is the exercise of any authority exterior to that of the ego. Far from settling questions of the rightful exercise of power of one person over another, the attitude engendered by a partial reading of Mill (or handed down as a kind of philosophical rumor) turns all human interactions into questions of power. This is particularly so for those who are, or feel themselves to be, at the lower end of the social scale. Their dignity as absolute sovereigns, as the Sun Kings of their own soul, is the most frequently infringed; life for them is a long series of acts of *lèse-majesté* by others. Their ego is like a wound that is never allowed to heal, that is constantly re-opened by reality, into which salt is ever rubbed by those with greater power and prestige than themselves.

16 | The Difficulty of Founding Common Decency on First Principles

ONE CAN SEE this in very small acts of rebellion against convention. On British trains, for example, young men and women often put their feet up on the seat opposite them if it is not occupied. Indeed, it is almost *de rigueur* for them to do so. As soon as they sit down, they put their feet up, as if marking their territory or claiming a right of conquest. They can hardly do it from mere weariness, for it is very unlikely that their legs are wearier than those of old ladies, who never put their feet up in this way.

Such is the absolute sovereignty of the individual over himself that very few people dare challenge them. To point out that the notice in the carriage says "Please do not put you feet up on the seats"—the kind of notice that only a few years ago would have seemed absurd, unnecessary, redundant—would be pointless, and perhaps even dangerous, since so many people now feel themselves obliged to defend their sovereignty with a knife. Indeed, the notice might be expected to provoke the very behavior it is intended to forestall, in so far as it constitutes an invitation for people to demonstrate the size of their character by an act of nonconformity.

Not long ago, a young woman on a train in which I was traveling ostentatiously put her feet up on the seat opposite her. She was clearly of the middle class, conformist non-conformity—or non-conformist conformity—long being a middle-class characteristic. Whatever the strictly scientific shortcomings of Lombroso's idea that criminality is inscribed biologically on the face, a glance at her was sufficient to re-assure me that she was unlikely to be a member of the knife-carrying community, and I asked her whether she would mind removing her feet from the seat. She at once (and without apparent acrimony) thought of a self-justification.

"My feet are clean," she said.

"Even so," I replied.

"They're not doing any harm," she countered.

Fortunately, she did then remove her feet from the seat, though I noticed that she put them on again as soon as I left the carriage at a station before hers. Our Socratic dialogue concerning the ethics of putting your feet up on a seat in a train was aborted.

However, had it continued, it is clear that all the argu-ments would have been on the young woman's side, at least if anything other than total, knock-down victory is a defeat for those who propose the maintenance of a particular stan-dard of conduct. She would, for example, have been able to ask for the evidence that the putting of feet up on unoccu-pied train seats was harmful to anybody. She had already claimed that her feet were clean, and it was therefore very unlikely that anyone's health would be compromised as a result of her behavior. Had anyone done the scientific experiment—that is to say, a double-blind trial—to establish whether feet on unoccupied trains seats harmed the people in any tangible way who later sat on them? Of course not, the very idea is absurd. Would the results of such a trial, if conducted, be published in *The New England Journal of*

Medicine, or even some less august journal of medical research? The question answers itself. But *prima facie* the likelihood of harm is slight, especially as every passenger wears protective clothing over that part of the anatomy that normally comes in contact with the seat. And the onus of proof rests, surely, on the person proposing to prohibit a certain kind of behavior. The young woman on the train might not actually have read her Mill, but she would know the argument, because almost everybody does.

Well then, putting your feet up on the seats is inelegant, though it might not be harmful to health. Ah, but who says so? Is it not a fact, both historical and anthropological, that what is and has been considered well-mannered behavior has varied or does vary according to time and place, and that what is or has been considered obligatory in one time and place is or has been viewed with absolute horror in others? Again, the young lady on the train might not have read Montaigne's essay on cannibals, in which he argues for the relativity of moral judgment, but she would have known the argument.

An appeal to democracy and majority opinion cannot work either, first because such majority opinion has no intrinsic right to impose itself upon minorities (quite the reverse, in fact), and second because even if majority opinion were relevant to the question, on *this* question majority opinion is almost certainly unknown. No one has ever conducted a survey to establish it, besides which it would be arguable as to which population's opinion should be canvassed. The population of the whole country? The population that travels on trains? That travels on particular train lines, whose opinion might vary from that of people who travel on different lines? That travels rarely, occasionally, often, or twice daily on trains? Should the opinion of someone who traveled only once in his lifetime on the train be counted equally with that of someone who went to work on it, and had done so for twenty years? Should the opinion of someone at the beginning of his career as a passenger count more than someone who is at the end of it, because the former has a greater interest in the future of trains?

It would be against the elementary principles of justice to argue that, if you allow people with clean feet to put them up on seats, people with dirty feet will soon follow suit. Even if we were to accept the argument as empirically correct, it would be unjust to penalize one person for his effect on the behavior of another, each person being totally responsible only for what he himself does.

In short, there is absolutely no conclusive reason why people should not put their feet up on occupied train seats, and no grounds for preventing them from doing so.

There is a great deal of everyday behavior, often thoughtlessly and prejudicially reprobated, of which the same might be said. What is wrong, for example, with littering the countryside? Who is actually harmed by it? The horrible aesthetic effect is no argument, because aesthetics are a matter of taste only, of opinion and not of fact, inherently indemonstrable to others. Mill specifically rejects such grounds for prohibiting anything. Moral disgust (whose metaphysical underpinnings, or lack thereof, are the same as those of aesthetic judgment), be it ever so strong, can never be the basis of prohibition. The disgusted person may expostulate and argue against, and avoid the company of, the person of whose conduct he disapproves, but he must not seek to change it by means of prohibition or legal sanctions. On this view, of course, even necrophilia would be permissible, since the only harm done by it would be the outrage to the feelings of those who are disgusted by it; but that counts for nothing, less than a feather in the balance.

17 | The Law of Conservation of
Righteous Indignation, and its
Connection to the Expansion of
Human Rights

THE ARGUMENTS ABOVE are always used only to
remove restraint, of course, never to encourage or establish
it. No one would think to ask a person who did not put his
feet up on the seat opposite him why he did not do so, or
engage him in a discussion as to why he did not do so. The
arguments are used only to render permissible the formerly
impermissible, except (perhaps) in one or two isolated
cases, for example smoking. There, a strange kind of moral
fervor supervenes, an illustration of a phenomenon akin to
a law of thermodynamics: namely, the law of the conserva-
tion of righteous indignation, which, if it does not attach to
one thing, will attach to another. It is as if the total fund of
such indignation is of constant size. As traditional moral
prohibitions, inhibitions, and considerations are destroyed
by the gnawing criticism of philosophical disputatiousness,
new ones rush in to fill the vacuum.

At first it seemed as if tobacco harmed mainly, or only,
the person who was foolish enough to smoke it; but this, of
course, would not have been sufficient grounds to harass
those who did so. This realization—one might surmise—
impelled research to demonstrate that smoking tobacco
(but not cannabis, for here the tide of opinion was in the

other direction) harmed third parties. More and more studies demonstrated more and more harms, until the point was reached at which even the furniture of rooms in which people had smoked became hazardous for infants, who absorbed noxious chemicals from wood and upholstery. This state of affairs justifies the most drastic regulations—perhaps one day the compulsory sterilization of smokers (remember that satire nowadays is prophecy). The desire to interfere in the lives of others is not automatically extinguished by reading Mill or by absorbing his opinions; indeed, it becomes more uncompromising with regard to those objects to which it becomes attached.

A change in the objects of our disapproval, however, is not merely a change of opinion; it can result in profound social changes. It turns everything that is not forbidden into a right, for obviously one has the right to do what no one has the right to prohibit. Suddenly, the world becomes filled with rights, and new ones are discovered every day, in the way that expeditions by entomologists to the Amazon basin discover new species of insect every day.

And people who are acutely aware of their own rights (other than such now-traditional ones as that to a fair trial and freedom from arbitrary arrest), and who have them present in their minds to the extent that they appeal to these rights at the first sign of frustration of their whims, tend for other reasons to be egotists of a radical hue. The metaphysical origin of their rights bothers them no more than the metaphysical origins of their belief in the existence of the Himalayas: the "thereness" of their rights and that of the Himalayas is equal. When George Leigh Mallory, the mountaineer, was asked why he wanted to climb Everest, he replied, "Because it is there." Rights are there in precisely the same way for those who want to exercise them.

Rights expand to meet the egos of those for whom freedom is nothing but unconstrained action. (The only good that deserves the name, says Mill, is that of pursuing our own good in our own way.)

Rights expand by two means. First, negative rights become positive rights. For example, the right of a woman to have a child, in the sense that no one has the power to prevent her if she so wishes, becomes the right to "possess" a child in actual fact, even at taxpayers' and society's expense. Infertility becomes an affront to or infringement on rights rather than a physiological misfortune, and since the technical means exist, so far very expensive and successful in only a small minority of cases, to correct that infertility, access to those means becomes itself a right, denial of which becomes a grounds of complaint and (more valuable still) of resentment. It goes without saying that any discrimination against women whatsoever on the evidence of their disposition, conduct, or lifestyle in their search for fertility treatment would likewise be an infringement on their right to a child. I want, therefore I have a right. In this dictum is contained the reason why it will prove so difficult in the long run to place any ethical boundaries upon technical advances in reproductive medicine; desire is sovereign, and rules in the Versailles of the mind. We affect to be appalled by the feticide practiced in India, but what objection can we really raise once we have accepted the majesty of the individual will?

The second means by which rights expand to meet the egos that demand them is by the denial of limiting reciprocity; the thinking goes that if a right is genuinely a right, it must be unconditional. The right to a fair trial cannot be abrogated by any other consideration, for example for reasons of state. Since this is the archetype of a human right, does it not follow that if I have a right to play my music, it likewise cannot be abrogated by any other consideration— for example that its volume prevents my neighbor from sleeping? Either I have a right or I don't; and since I do, it is hard luck on the insomniac neighbor who wants to be refreshed by sleep before he returns to work in the morning.

Needless to say, my neighbor believes that he has a right, equally unconditional, to play his music. The ensuing clash of rights can be resolved only by appeal to force in their defense.

This is not merely hypothetical, or a construct of my imagination. In my career as a doctor I several times saw people severely injured as a result of the clash of rights, as well as prisoners driven to extreme measures by their neighbor's assumed right to listen to music at high volume in the early hours of every morning. These prisoners were not violent people by inclination, but since the authorities had vacated their powers of adjudication and enforcement, nothing was left except the argument of the club and the knife.

18 | The Paradox of Radical Individualism Leading to Authoritarianism

A PHILOSOPHY THAT sets out to destroy the influence of custom, tradition, authority, and prejudice does indeed destroy particular customs, traditions, authorities, and prejudices, but only to replace them by others. The new, in this aspect of human existence as in all others, may be better than the old, but it may also be worse. Improvement has to start somewhere, but so does deterioration. The philosophy—or perhaps attitude would be a better word to describe it—of radical individualism instills a deep prejudice in favor of oneself and one's own ego, and in the process establishes customs that are social only in the sense that many people have them, and customs only in the sense that they will encourage conduct that will survive from generation to generation if uninterrupted. Life is conceived of as a limitless extension of consumer choice, a trawl around the existential supermarket, from whose shelves lifestyles can be picked up as are brands of processed food, and with no deeper or more meaningful consequences. As one French supermarket chain puts it, *le client est roi*, the customer is king, though of course when the customer wants assistance with something, he will be hard put to find anyone to help him. The customer is king all right, but only of himself.

Such radical individualism has another paradoxical effect: what starts out as a search for increased if not total individualism, ends up by increasing the power of government over individuals. It does not do so by the totalitarian method of rendering compulsory all that is not forbidden— a process that in all human history has gone farthest, perhaps, in North Korea—but by destroying all moral authority that intervenes between individual human will and governmental power. Everything that is not forbidden by law is, *ipso facto*, permissible. What is legally permissible is morally permissible. "There is no law against it" becomes an unanswerable justification for conduct that is selfish and egotistical.

This, of course, makes the law, and therefore those who make the law, the moral arbiters of society. It is they who, by definition, decide what is permissible and what is not. All stigma is removed from conduct that is too expressly and actively forbidden.

Given the nature of human nature, it hardly needs pointing out that those who are delegated the job of moral arbiter for the whole of society enjoy their power and come to think that they deserve it, that they have been chosen for their special insight into the way life should be lived. It is not only legislators who succumb to this temptation, but judges also, and who can blame them, if there is no other source of collective authority? Radical individualism is thus not only compatible with the radical centralization of authority, but is a product of it. The individual is left to live his life as his whim dictates, but the central power gratefully accepts the power-generating responsibility of protecting him from the consequences of doing so.

If anything is addictive, prescriptive power is addictive. Once you have it (at any rate if you are so inclined by temperament) you can never have enough of it. The lack of any intervening authority between the individual on the one hand, and the sovereign political power on the other, enables the latter to insinuate itself into the smallest crevices of daily life. An infinite power comes to think of itself as infinitely good because it is infinitely responsible for the welfare of its subjects (who, not surprisingly, soon become objects of its ministrations). Decision-making divides into two spheres: the serious business of life is left to the sovereign authority, while the individual is left to his own Brownian motion in an ever more compressed space. Recently, for example, I wanted to have the windows of a house cleaned. They had been cleaned for years by a father-and-son team with whose services I was more than satisfied. But suddenly the government decided that it was too dangerous for men to climb up ladders, at least for so trivial a purpose, with the result that I had to clean the windows myself by leaning out of them in a most dangerous fashion, thus depriving the window-cleaners of a living.

The lack of intervening authorities, such as family, church, professional organizations, etc., accustoms us to expect, and accept, the central direction of our lives, even when it results in absurdities. And thus the corporatization of society proceeds *pari passu* with the extension of unbridled egotism.

19 | Racial Discrimination Being Bad, All Discrimination Is Bad

NOTHING IS DEEMED worse about prejudice and pre-conceived ideas than that they lead to discrimination. The career of the word discrimination in my lifetime has been an interesting and revealing one. In the early days of my schooling, it meant to make a proper judgment—aesthetic, moral, and intellectual—and my teachers were possibly the last generation of pedagogues who believed that the inculcation of powers of discrimination was the noblest part of their job, so that some of their pupils, at least, might come to appreciate, and if possible add to, the finest traditions and achievements of our civilization. (I was far more refractory to this high-mindedness than I should have been, to my everlasting but now impotent regret.)

Accordingly, a person who did not discriminate, who was undiscriminating, was a person without taste, morality, or intellect; undiscriminating, he was likely to be indiscriminate in his behavior. Discrimination was for these teachers the most important function of the mind; without it, truth could not be distinguished from falsehood, beauty from ugliness, or good from evil, and the purpose of pedagogy was to instill the correct prejudices. In the field of aesthetics, all that is necessary for kitsch to triumph is for men to fail to discriminate.

The primary meaning of the word has changed since then. If one could have administered a word-association test years ago, offering discrimination as the word to provoke associations, the list would probably have read intelligence, connoisseurship, sensitivity, powers of observation, acuity, correct judgment, and so forth. Such a test would yield a very different list nowadays. It would probably include redneck, bigot, racist, homophobe, reactionary, and (worst of all) conservative. Images of lynching would perhaps flicker across the cinema screen of the mind's eye, if I may put it thus without offending the cognitive scientists.

One of the problems with changes in the meanings of words is that new connotations can often contaminate or overwhelm old denotations. If I say that I am in favor of discrimination in the first sense, I will probably be taken really to mean, if only sub- or unconsciously (my protests to the contrary notwithstanding), discrimination in the second sense. Whatever I say will not avail me, for other people will claim to know my meaning better than I know it myself.

Hence the very act of distinguishing between higher and lower, better and worse, deeper and shallower, becomes suspect and best avoided. A man who judges books, art, music, philosophy, and science *sub specie æternitatis* thus becomes, in the imagination of many, a man who would join a lynch mob, because he hates, fears, and despises black men. He needn't open his mouth on the subject of race relations; his preference for what he believes to be better rather than worse, or higher rather than lower, condemn him out of hand, without need of trial. He is an Enemy of the People.

This is not to say, of course, that prejudiced discrimination in the second sense has not existed or does not exist. Just a few examples—I will avoid the usual ones—will suffice to prove the point. Blacks in Moscow risk assault, especially

if they are in the company of Russian women. In the area of
the British city in which I worked, a Sikh boy who went out
with a Muslim girl risked violence from her brothers. Indian
women in search of a husband, especially in the north of the
country, still prefer a light complexion to a dark one.

None of this is very glorious, and an almost infinite
number of other examples could no doubt be given. And
because such prejudiced discrimination has often led to the
most horrifying outbreak of intercommonned violence, and
even to genocide, even though for long periods of time is
compatible with social peace, it is believed, by those who
feel compelled to exhibit their opposition to genocide, that
we should clear our minds of all prejudice whatsoever, in
case it should suddenly turn genocidal. (Here it may interest
readers to know that visitors to the United States are asked
to answer, by means of ticking a yes-or-no box on their
landing cards, whether they have ever participated in or
committed an act of genocide, a question I imagine even the
most committed genocidal maniac has little difficulty
answering correctly, at least from the point of view of gain-
ing entry to the country. The cross-cultural existence of the
official mind is, perhaps, evidence also of the existence a
universal human nature.)

Virtuous people the world over, or at least in that part of
the world susceptible to moral enthusiasms and the pleasures of guilt, try to expunge their minds of all prejudice, and
go out into the world each morning with a freshly minted
mind, a *tabula rasa*, from which all previous knowledge and
experience of people and things have been eliminated. It is
as if the virtuous life required that each moment should be
lived as though the world had been created anew, and no

moment had any connection with any other moment— every minute, every second, every fraction of a second being ontologically separate. In some ways, no doubt, it is indeed a great virtue to retain one's ability to be surprised anew by the world, and not to be so ground down by experience and weariness of the flesh that the world appears flat and un- profitable. But if we met a man who expressed astonishment that it was colder in January than in July, and insisted upon drawing our attention to this amazing fact, we should think him at least a fool, and possibly a madman. The best way to be a bore, said Voltaire, is to say everything—that is, to assume that nothing can be taken for granted. A man who leaves nothing out is, in the end, a man who says nothing.

Rejection of Prejudice
Not a Good in Itself

THIS IS NOT really the place to rehearse the arguments as
to whether or not Man has innate ideas, or a fixed nature
that makes him inclined to one thing rather than another,
by biological fatality, as it were. To do so would be virtually
to write a history of Western philosophy, and perhaps of
other philosophical traditions as well. I shall mention only a
few strains of thought, not meaning to provide a comprehensive list.

Socrates, at least as portrayed in the dialogues of Plato,
draws the truth out of his various interlocutors, very often
without propounding a doctrine of his own. The assumption is that the truth is within everyone from the first, and is
not discovered in the way that Columbus discovered America, or in the way that a new species of frog is discovered in
the Amazonian jungle. The philosopher is an archaeologist
of knowledge, rather than a builder of it: he strips away the
misconceptions that have accreted since birth (an idea that
Wittgenstein, generally regarded as the greatest philosopher of the twentieth century, also propagated).

Perhaps I may give an example, from my (admittedly
unusual) clinical practice, of how knowledge or awareness
may be implicit. I worked part of my time as a doctor in a
prison, and sometimes prisoners would tell me—often in
the hope of obtaining tranquilizers, one of the currencies of

prison—that if they met a sex-offender in the prison they would feel obliged to kill him. It seems almost a universal human nature that sex-offenders are everywhere the object of the scorn of prisoners.

I would ask a prisoner who came to me in this fashion why he felt so obliged, and the dialogue would run more or less along the following course:

"Because they interfere with little kiddies."

"And do you have any children yourself?" I would ask.

"Three," he would reply.

"By how many mothers?"

"Three," he would say.

"And do you still see any of your children?"

"No," he would say.

"Why not?"

"Because her new boyfriend doesn't want me to," he would say.

"And probably the mother of your children will have more than one new boyfriend in the coming years?"

"Yes," he would say.

"And how will one or more of her boyfriends treat your children?"

The point was made. Although not well-educated, the prisoner was well able to grasp the full implication of his reply. (I have never been much struck by the supposedly low intelligence of prisoners, which supposedly makes them incapable of understanding the meaning of their own conduct, and which therefore makes them little more, from the point of view of moral responsibility, than minors.) The fact that the prisoner admitted that he had created the very conditions in which children were most likely to be abused, physically or sexually or both, and that the admission had been extracted from him by very simple questions to which he himself gave the answers, with little prompting and with the addition of no new information, suggested to him that he had been culpably complicit in the commission of precisely the kind of crimes whose perpetrators he now wished to punish extrajudicially. The situation casts an interesting sidelight, incidentally, on prisoners' own view of the efficacy and justice of punishment. In order not to leave him desolate, I would tell him that though the past cannot be undone, the future was yet to be made, and that he could at least ensure that he never again brought into the world a child whom he would abandon to the abusers. Almost heartbreakingly, he would confess that all he had ever really wanted was the kind of stable and "conventional" family that he himself had never known, of whose pre-conditions he had not the faintest notion.

Our little dialogue established to his own satisfaction that his conduct (and that of the mothers of his children) had been wrong, and that, in his heart of hearts, he had always known it to be wrong. If we continued the dialogue, we would reach, by the same method, conclusions that were both obvious and revelatory (an odd combination of qualities). We would discover that all human wishes and desires, even if simultaneously existent in the same breast, were not mutually compatible, and that the fulfillment of every wish or desire entailed the frustration of another: in other words, that having a life of pleasure without a remainder of frustration was impossible, and that it was always necessary to choose between different pleasures and their accompanying or consequent frustrations. We desire both security and excitement, but cannot have both at the same time, because excitement is impossible without uncertainty, and security is impossible with it. We want both sexual liberty and the exclusive sexual possession of another, but we cannot have both, at least not if many other people want the same thing, and not without a liberal dose of hypocrisy, which in some circumstances may be, if not a virtue exactly, then the least harmful of several possible alternative vices.

At any rate, the prisoner would understand without difficulty that to abandon children is wrong (if anything is wrong), and that at least some of his travails derived from a failure to act on the understanding—which, in the Socratic sense, had always been present in him—that there were inherent limitations to the satisfaction of appetites. He would understand that having it all, and having it now, is simply not a human possibility, and that to behave as if it were leads to disaster, both for the individual and for society.

What would have enabled the prisoner to act upon this instinctive but sophisticated appreciation that pleasure cannot be unmixed, or rights enjoyed without duties performed, if not prejudice and social pressure for him to conform to certain indisputable standards? Such social pressure is the result not of thousands or millions of people having thought and reasoned about the matter from first principles, and by force of argument having come to the same conclusion. It is from social prejudice that one learns social virtue. Metaphysical thought and reflection come later.

Nothing is easier, of course, than to demonstrate that the kind of social prejudice to which I refer can sometimes, or often, lead to terrible manifestations of bigotry and its associated cruelty. The reader, I am sure, could furnish many examples of his own; the history of the world, alas, furnishes a lot of material in this regard. But it is one thing to say that this or that prejudice is disgusting or extremely harmful, and another to say that we can do without prejudice altogether. There are surgical operations often performed in the past that did more harm than good, and no doubt this is still the case, but there is no reason why mankind should forego the life-saving advantages of surgery as a matter of principle.

As is so often, though not always, the case, Doctor Johnson has something profound to say on the matter. Nothing could be further removed from modern sensibility, with its insistence that at each moment, at each junction in the road of life, each individual must stand alone as a totally original self-creation, than Doctor Johnson's combination of ruthless honesty, profound introspection, and deep common sense. No one could suspect Doctor Johnson himself of a lack of individuality, or of blind conformity; indeed, it would be difficult to think of any more distinctive individual than he. Yet in his life of Jonathan Swift, Doctor Johnson takes the Dean to task for his self-conscious and willful eccentricity of person and opinion.

Singularity [writes Doctor Johnson], as it implies a contempt of the general practice, is a kind of defiance which justly provokes the hostility of ridicule; he, therefore, who indulges in peculiar traits is worse than others, if he be not better.

It is worth noting that Doctor Johnson, while conservative, is not reactionary. He is not suggesting that no improvement of manners or opinions is possible, or that any deviation from the beliefs and practices of the past is inherently reprehensible. He does, however, raise a possibility that reformers of many kinds have been unwilling to contemplate: that change can be for the worse as well as for the better, and that the will to originality and to judge everything by the light of one's own unaided opinion can be more a manifestation of a malign egotism than of a desire for truth or the good life. Of course, the desire for truth can be, perhaps always is, alloyed with the satisfaction of the ego. We no longer believe in the lonely, disinterested searcher after scientific truth in the Book of Nature, who has no personal ambition to satisfy, even if it is only to immortalize himself (how much less scientific research would be published if it were done only anonymously). Yet if we do not believe in the existence of people wholly without ego, we do still believe in the existence of people who are overwhelmingly driven by ego to the exclusion of almost everything else.

Rejection of prejudice and received ideas can be good, therefore, but it is not good in itself.

21 | The Impossibility of the Mind as a Blank Slate

MANY PHILOSOPHERS, and increasingly neurobiologists, have doubted the *tabula rasa* theory of mind, according to which the brain acts (or in an ideal world cleansed of pre-conceptions and prejudices, possibly could act) purely as a calculator on the basis of the evidence passively presented to it. In fact, the *tabula rasa* was never very realistic. Given the relative size of man and that of the environment in which he lives and takes his being, a selection of attention was always necessary; only the mind of God could attend equally to everything at once.

Now, either the selection of attention is random, or it is not. But randomness of the matters to be attended to is inherently unlikely, if for no other reason than that it would not be very good for survival. If man had been disinclined by nature to distinguish between a lion's roar and the sound of his own footfall, it is unlikely that he would ever have left the savannah (or even have reached it). In other words, man, like other creatures, must be born with *de facto* prejudices.

Of course, these prejudices—hard-wired, in current terminology—are not in the form of propositions, such as that all Jews are avaricious or all Muslims fanatical. Even Kant's analysis of the necessity (that is to say, of the philosophical or metaphysical, not the social necessity) for *a priori* ideas that are not mere logical truisms does not suggest that these ideas operate in most people's minds by means of propositions consciously adopted and accepted as true. These *a priori* ideas, which in Kant's view are a precondition of any thought at all, can be put in propositional form; but Kant never suggested that, until he did so, no human being had ever thought.

Many other thinkers have considered the question of the propensities or prejudices with which Man comes into the world. Adam Smith, for example, who is sometimes taken as the apostle of selfishness, was a moral philosopher before he was a political economist, and he erected a system of morality based upon Man's inherent propensity to sympathize with other men. "Every man whatsoever," he states at the beginning of *The Theory of Moral Sentiments*, partakes of this sympathy.

According to Smith, it was from this brute fact of human nature—a fortunate fact, but a brute one nonetheless—that all morality ultimately derived. He wrote seventy years before the British alienist and anthropologist J. C. Prichard first drew attention to what he called moral insanity (or what, until a few years ago, was called psychopathy, before it became sociopathy, antisocial personality disorder, and then dissocial personality disorder, without any increase in real understanding), a condition in which a person appears to be utterly without the sympathy for others that Smith declares to be universal. This, however, would have altered Smith's view but slightly, for Prichard's moral insanity was either congenital or acquired by injury to the brain—in other words, was itself a prejudice (or absence thereof), which demonstrated that morality was a natural and not a metaphysical, much less a supernatural, phenomenon.

More recently, the philosopher of science, Karl Popper, who was most famous for his falsifiability criterion of scientific and non-scientific theories, denied that there could be any pre-theoretical perceptions, let alone statements. In other words, every perception, and every statement about the world, had built-in prejudices in the nature of theoretical presuppositions, even if these prejudices were unconscious and unacknowledged. In Popper's view, such prejudice was always corrigible—though presumably only by other evidence that was equally theory-laden—but you could never get to a truth that was free of presuppositions. Whether or not he was right in this, it does seem as if the quest for what positivist philosophers once called sensibilia—the elementary, undifferentiated, and featureless atoms of sensory experience, from which the whole of human knowledge was supposed ultimately to be composed—was ill-conceived, and now well and truly over. Research in the 1950s and '60s by the Nobel Prize-winning neurophysiologists Hubel and Wiesel on the visual cortex of the cat established that neurons were differentially predisposed to react to different stimuli in the environment. Furthermore, neural plasticity declined with age.

Even if it is true that we are born with certain predispositions, prejudices, presuppositions, and propensities, however, it does not follow that our lives are predestined or predetermined, for they can work themselves out in an infinite variety of ways. No one supposes that a man's inborn capacity for language determines what he will actually say; whatever is inborn is not like liquid in a bottle, incompressible. The hydraulic notion of human emotion has long been a favorite of those who deny the need for self-control. They believe that a man is not only born with a capacity for violence and aggression, but has a fixed quantity of them within him, which must be expressed in one way or another, at least if that person is not to implode or explode. Perhaps the *ne plus ultra* of this belief was the statement of a man who had just murdered his lover: "I had to kill her, doctor, or I don't know what I would have done."

The hydraulic notion—in the propagation of which a debased Freudianism has no doubt played a large part—ignores the effect of habit not only on the outward expression of emotion, but on the actual experience of emotion. A man who habitually expressed rage in an uninhibited fashion would soon find himself enraged by everything. Those who believed that every man had a fixed quantity of aggression within him, believed as a consequence that the dissemination of violent imagery, in films and on television, would lead to a decline in actual violence, since the violence within each man would be discharged (like static electricity, to change the physical metaphor) by means of catharsis. The evidence, admittedly, suggests otherwise. It is true that fully grown adults do not become more violent as a result of watching violence on a screen; but those who watch such violence from an early age *are* more inclined to violent behavior than those who do not. What was hoped to be cathartic is actually provocative.

Of course, we are dealing with statistical generalizations and not one-to-one correspondences. Even in the worst of societies, not everyone is bad. Not all, not most, children will become violent under the influence of screen violence. The only society known to me of which it was claimed that almost everyone was irredeemably bad, cruel, vindictive, and callous was that of the Ik, a Ugandan tribe described in his book, *The Mountain People*, by the anthropologist Colin Turnbull. This primitive tribe—if one is still permitted to use such a term—was forced by a variety of circumstances to leave its ancestral home and live in an inhospitable and unaccustomed landscape. As a result, the members of the tribe became totally egotistical, because they were concerned only for their own personal survival. Here, truly, was a Hobbesian world, in which life was a war of each against all. Sons laughed at the death of their mother, where they did not actually help to bring it about; fathers watched their sons starve to death, with equanimity or even enjoyment. The suffering of others was the greatest, the only, source of fun for the Ik. Turnbull, unusually for an anthropologist, came to hate the people whom he was studying.

Here, it seemed, were a people who had lost their prejudices and pre-conceived ideas as to what was right and wrong. The result was not edifying.

22 | The Ideal of Equality of Opportunity Necessary to a World Without Prejudice

IN DUE COURSE Turnbull, now dead, was accused of inaccuracy by other anthropologists. They, who perhaps were more wedded to the idea of the noble savage than he, and were therefore more inclined to be skeptical of descriptions of the ignobility of savages, said that Turnbull did not speak the Ik language, and therefore misinterpreted what he witnessed. Far from being the inhuman monsters depicted by him, the Ik were actually sweet-tempered, compassionate, and lovable. This divergence of opinion seems almost incredible; but if his critics were right, Turnbull had libeled an entire tribe, amongst whom he claimed not to have seen one act of kindness.

Even as a mere thought experiment, however, or fictional dystopia, Turnbull's book is interesting and instructive. What would a society be like in which people had entirely lost their prejudices in favor of those traditionally called their "nearest and dearest"? In fact, this is the kind of society that some rationalist moral philosophers would recommend, the most famous of those now living being Professor Singer of Princeton, who first came to international prominence with his book *Animal Liberation*. Singer has since gone on to advocate infanticide in selected cases, arguing that sufficiently disabled human beings are less worthy of moral consideration and the protection of the law than certain animals.

In the eyes of rationalists, all people are not only born equal but must be treated equally. This equality of treatment must not be formal only—equality under the law—but must result in equality of outcome, for if it does not, the proclaimed equality is bogus. It is, after all, an undeniable fact that in many situations a millionaire will be treated very differently, with more consideration and deference, than a pauper. The only way to ensure that no such difference persists is by ensuring that henceforth there are no more millionaires and no more paupers.

Unfortunately, differentiation into classes begins at birth, or even before. (For the sake of the argument, it doesn't really matter whether society is divided into clearly demarcated classes or whether there is merely a gradient from lowest to highest. All that matters is that there should be inequality, as obviously there is in all present-day societies, even the most egalitarian of them.) There is a statistical tendency, even in the most socially mobile and meritocratic of modern societies, for people to end up in the hierarchy not very far from where they were born, notwithstanding many exceptions. For egalitarians, then, it is not enough that there should be no legal barriers or impediments to social mobility—in either direction, of course, though social descent is a phenomenon less studied than ascent. (It is important to remember that one man's ascent is not necessarily another's descent, except in a society of courtiers.)

Egalitarians may deny that they desire exact equality of outcome, but they have great difficulty in specifying exactly what degree of inequality is acceptable to them. That is why there are so many studies that examine inequality, whether of income or of some other marker, and why any increase in inequality is lamented as evidence in itself that an injustice has been committed. This, no doubt, is why you never see an increase in inequality praised as representing an increase in justice, as it might be—I do not say must be—if justice has anything to do with the rewards and penalties for individual conduct.

It would not be too much to say that in my own field, medicine, there has developed an obsession with inequality of outcome as a good in itself. Scarcely a week goes by in which the medical journals do not call upon governments to institute the most drastic action because some groups of people enjoy much better health than others. For example, in developed countries such as Britain, the infant mortality rate (the number of children per thousand live births who die before they are one year old) of the poorest section of the population is double that of the richest. Rich adults also live longer and healthier lives than do poor ones, and only half the difference is attributable to bad habits such as smoking. Since the most fundamental of human rights is that to life itself, it follows that a difference in life expectancy— accompanied as it always is by differences in morbidity, there being very few acute or chronic diseases to which the poor are not more susceptible than the rich—is a denial of a basic human right, and ought to be eliminated.

If equality were a desirable goal in itself, however, it would be a matter of indifference whether equality of life expectancy were achieved by causing the poor to live longer or the rich to die sooner. Of course, hatred of the rich is a much stronger emotion than love of the poor: no rampaging mobs ever went through a city seeking out the poor to whom they could give away their possessions. But whatever bitterness or resentment he might hide in his heart, no respectable public health doctor has ever sought to promote the death of the rich as a way to achieve equality in life expectancy. The way forward is to bring the poor up to the standards of the rich, even if in practice this means expropriating the rich by means of taxation.

Recent attempts to bring about equality, however, both economic and social, have not been wholly happy; indeed, they have resulted in some of the worst atrocities in the history of mankind. The most radical such attempt was that of the Khmer Rouge in Cambodia; the Shining Path of Peru would have committed similar atrocities, but on a much larger scale, had they not been defeated. It is an open question whether, behind the urge to equality, lies the urge to power; all one can say is that, whenever the urge expresses itself in an uncompromising way, it leads to the utmost horror.

Political ideals, or at least names of ideals, die hard; people are reluctant to give up what they once thought was a good idea. And so the ideal of equality was reinvented as the ideal of equality of opportunity. No one should be born with a different chance of succeeding in life merely by virtue of an accident of birth. And for a society to exist in which there were equality of opportunity, the elimination of prejudice—including that in favor of one's own children—would be required.

23 | Equality of Opportunity Inherently Totalitarian

UNFORTUNATELY, this ideal, if taken seriously, that is to say literally, is scarcely less horrible in its implications than that of equality of outcome. No reflection is necessary to realize that parents are very different in important qualities that are likely, though not certain, to influence their children. Some parents are highly cultivated and have beautiful manners, while others regard all forms of academic achievement as pointless or worse, and are extremely boorish. (The cultivated can be boorish, of course, and the uneducated well-mannered.)

Despite technological advances, the human mind lies beyond our understanding and remains incalculable: a boorish father does not necessarily make a boorish son, or a well-mannered one a well-mannered son. It is one of the glories of the possession of consciousness that human beings are able to reflect upon both precept and example, and change themselves accordingly. Many of my patients explain their bad behavior, for example their violence to women, by the fact that they had witnessed such behavior at home from the earliest age; others recoiled in horror from the very idea of violence to women for precisely the same reason.

Still, it can hardly be denied that, *grosso modo*, the facts of where and when and into what kind of environment one is born have an effect upon one's subsequent life, including the path one takes. It could scarcely be otherwise. It has been one of the great mistakes of contemporary social thought, at least as exemplified by the policies pursued by governments, that the most important aspect of the environment into which children are born, which most influences their chances in life, is the material or economic aspect. The absence of some physical appurtenance has been regarded as a terrible deprivation, while moral squalor and emotional instability had been attributed to material poverty alone. The solution that suggests itself, then, is the improvement of the material circumstances into which children are born, until such time as they are equal.

However, people who think like this do so because they have asked the wrong question, or looked down the wrong end of the telescope. They have asked where poverty comes from instead of where wealth comes from. You might as well ask how ignorance of cardiac surgery ever came into being, rather than knowledge of it, as if cardiac surgery were an activity natural to man in his most primitive state. If you continue to find poverty puzzling, you will be led sooner or later to the conclusion that poverty is caused by wealth. In a sense, this is true: a man with assets of $100 million is relatively poor in the company of men with assets of $1000 million. But wealth as such, the wresting of increasing luxury from the materials of nature, cannot rest upon poverty. Even wealth that is extracted from slave labor derives from a foundation of ideas, not only about the social acceptability of slave labor, but about what and how goods are to be produced. No one would have raised cotton by slave labor unless someone knew how to spin it. Even in the worst of systems, something other than exploitation is necessary to the production of wealth. The worst that plunder and mere exploitation can do is to destroy wealth or inhibit its growth; they cannot create wealth, except for some individuals. When Bill Gates founded Microsoft, whom did he impoverish, by subsequently becoming the richest man in the world? Certainly not me: though my wealth is but a tiny fraction of his, yet it is larger than it would have been without him.

It is simply not plausible to suggest that our economic system, imperfect as it no doubt is, rests upon a foundation of exploitation and plunder; yet, the life chances of people within it remain unequal. How is this to be explained?

In the city in which I once worked, there was a most conspicuous and obvious fact: the children of Sikh and Hindu immigrants moved up rapidly in society. By contrast, the poor whites, with whom for a time they shared the impoverished and run-down urban areas, stagnated. They were, of course, richer than they would once have been, but only because society as a whole was much richer.

What accounted for the difference between the children of these immigrants on the one hand, and those of the natives on the other? The immigrants, after all, arrived with certain disadvantages. They were very poor, at least by the standards of the country in which they arrived; many did not speak the language, or speak it well. They were neither skilled nor well-educated. They were not particularly welcome to the general population. Indeed, they were imposed upon the population by a government (whose members would not have to live with the day-to-day consequences of the policy) that saw them as an answer to a particular economic problem, namely a shortage of cheap labor. Gestures and even acts of hostility towards them were not uncommon.

And yet they flourished, as the host population (relatively speaking) did not. Why?

They had two, or possibly three, great advantages *vis-à-vis* the local population. The first is that they had a strong collective prejudice in favor of the importance of the family. This prejudice, which had been under strong and prolonged ideological attack in the West, no longer existed among the local population. It had been replaced by another prejudice, that all forms of family life—a constantly shifting cast of presences in the household among them—were morally, emotionally, and socially equal. It is, in general, far easier to replace a good prejudice by a bad one than the other way around, perhaps (here I speak as a person without religious belief) because the heart of man is inclined more to evil than to good, to gluttony more than to moderation, to hate more than to love, to sloth more than to industry, to pride more than to modesty, and so forth.

Yet while a strong attachment to family is probably a necessary condition of social success on a large scale (that is to say, not on a purely individual scale, for we are talking in generalities, not absolutes), it is almost certainly not sufficient. It is also necessary that the people in question believe in the value of effort and education, and that they live in sufficiently open a society that such effort and education will, or at least might, triumph over obstacles, such as the prejudice of others. And since such a valuable belief is held more by some groups than by others, it is more likely to be a prejudice than a deeply considered opinion based upon a careful examination of the evidence.

The poor whites were of a different opinion: they lived in so unjust and sclerotic a society that nothing they did would improve their condition or raise them on the social scale. Needless to say, this was not an attitude that led to much in the way of constructive striving. I will not remark on the psychologically comforting nature of such an attitude or belief, or how it both explains and excuses failure in advance of all experience, and permits people to warm themselves with the idea that, but for injustice, their lives would have been very different from what they are. It is an idea that is largely taken for granted.

Evidence can, of course, be adduced for all the prejudices that account for the different trajectories of the two groups, but it is doubtful whether any evidence does or could amount to a knock-down argument in their favor, forcing an abandonment of the opposite prejudices by those who have them. So long as the Indian immigrants are upwardly mobile and the natives socially immobile, both groups will be able to point to the evidence from their own experience in favor of their world outlook. It will always be possible for a believer in the injustice of society to point to cases of unrewarded merit; likewise, it will always be possible for believers in the value of personal effort to point to cases of triumph in the face of the most severe adversity. It is the world outlook that determines the evidence, not the other way round.

Now, if it is accepted that a preconceived or inherited world outlook affects important aspects of behavior, which themselves affect a person's life chances, as much as or even more than his initial position on the economic scale, it follows for true believers in equality of opportunity that inherited world outlooks must be equalized. And the only possible way of doing so would be to ensure than no children grew up with prejudices different from those of any other, and to instill all children, not with no prejudices, for such would be impossible, but with the same prejudices. And to do this would require methods of the kind described in Aldous Huxley's *Brave New World*. The achievement of equality of opportunity, which would require the elimination of prejudicial prejudices, would necessitate a totalitarian dictatorship more terrifyingly thoroughgoing than any yet seen. It would make the achievement of equality of outcome, at least in material terms, seem like an exercise in liberty.

It is not an unreasonable or impossible goal to establish a society in which nobody is denied opportunity because of formal barriers; but a society so free from prejudice that parents were not permitted to be more concerned for the welfare of their own children than for anyone (or everyone) else's, and actually felt no greater such concern, would be horrible beyond powers of description. Prejudice is necessary for the maintenance of the most elementary decency.

24 | The Rejection of Authority as Egotism

THE IDEAL OF life without prejudices, stereotypes, pre-conceptions, and pre-existing authority is nevertheless regarded as a proper, indeed a noble one. Our own moral authority in everything should be our goal. This is not a new idea: in the middle of the nineteenth century, the Russian novelist, Ivan Turgenev, coined the term *nihilism* for it. In *Fathers and Sons*, published in 1861, the character Yevgeny Bazarov rejects all inherited authority or belief, in favor of those things that he can either prove with his own eyes, or deduce from facts known to him.

Bazarov is a man of a new type in Russia. For the first time in Russian history, university education is spreading beyond the very restricted circle of the gentry and aristocracy. Bazarov, a medical student, believes in science and in nothing but science. He goes on a visit to the home of the parents of his friend and disciple, Arkady Kirsanov, who are small gentry landowners. Arkady's uncle, Pavel Kirsanov, is an aristocrat of the old school, who takes an immediate dislike to Bazarov.

"And this Monsieur Bazarov, what is he exactly?" he [Pavel Kirsanov] inquired with deliberation.
    "He is a nihilist," replied Arkady.

"A what?" asked Nikolai Petrovich [Arkady's father and Pavel's brother].

"He is a nihilist," repeated Arkady.

"A nihilist," said Nikolai Petrovich. "That comes from the Latin, *nihil*—nothing, I imagine, the term must signify a man who . . . who recognizes nothing?"

"Say—who respects nothing," put in Pavel Petrovich. . .

"Who looks at everything critically," observed Arkady.

"Isn't that exactly the same thing?" asked Pavel Petrovich.

"No, it's not the same thing. A nihilist is a person who does not take any principle for granted, however much the principle may be revered."

A little further on in the novel, Uncle Pavel interrogates both Arkady and Bazarov himself:

"I fail to understand you. . . . How you can decline to recognize principles and precepts passes my comprehension. What other basis for conduct in life have we got?"

"I've told you already, uncle, that we don't recognize any authorities," Arkady interposed.

"We base our conduct on what we recognize as useful," Bazarov went on. "In these days, the most useful thing we can do is repudiate—and so we repudiate."

"Everything?"

"Everything."

Bazarov comes to a sticky end: he catches typhus from a peasant who died of it, and upon whom he performs an unnecessary autopsy. He dies before he can fully understand the aridity of his scorched earth approach to life.

Bazarov's attitude of repudiation—what I suppose would once have been called spiritual pride—is now, if not a mass phenomenon, a very widespread one. I experienced a striking instance of it on a flight to Dublin from England. Next to me sat a young Irish social worker, who noticed that I was reading a famous book, *Obedience to Authority* by Stanley Milgram, the famous American social psychologist who died young, in part from refusal to alter his living habits. In his book, Milgram describes the experiments he conducted to demonstrate that ordinary people would, without any compulsion except the presence of a figure supposedly in authority, electrocute a complete stranger. The social worker said to me that, having grown up in Ireland under the iron tutelage of the Catholic Church, she was against all forms of authority.

"All forms?" I asked.

"All forms," she replied. She had precisely the "indescribable composure" that Turgenev says is possessed by Bazarov.

"So you don't mind," I asked, "if I now go to the cockpit of this aircraft and take over the controls?"

This, it turned out (I think because it was a matter of her life and death), was a completely different matter. The authority of the pilot was based upon knowledge, experience, and proper certification.

"And who," I asked, "certifies his knowledge and experience?"

The answer was obvious: people with even greater knowledge and experience. But surely, I asked, this must lead to an infinite regress that, in this imperfect world of ours, would have to stop somewhere? Of course, but the state had looked into all that, and decided who constituted the competent authority. But from where did the state gain its authority? We, the people, of course. But who gave us, the people, authority? Well, it is so inscribed in the Book of Nature. This being the case, how is it that it was discovered so late in the history of humanity? How come it was not evident to Shakespeare, Newton, and Bach, who were at least as gifted as we?

These were deep questions for a short flight. But it was clear to me that the person who was against all authority was against only some authority, the authority she disliked. The one authority she really respected, of course, was her own.

25 | Prejudice a Requirement of Benevolence

THE DESIRE OR moral imperative to live without prejudice or stereotypes has become widespread. Negative stereotypes in particular give rise to guilty feeling: no one would worry unduly that he thought old ladies with arthritis and blue-rinsed hair were unlikely to rob him in the street.

It is negative stereotypes that bother us and put our thoughts in a whirl. There have been so many negative stereotypes that have been false, demeaning, and cruel, and that were made a justification for injustice or barbarity, that the very idea of stereotyping any group negatively has been discredited. Not so very long ago, the Chinese were regarded by many Westerners as sunk in lethargy, by nature so mentally torpid that they would never emerge from their backwardness. Now, if anything, the prejudice has turned 180 degrees: the Chinese work so hard that they sleep little and are likely, through their superior mental equipment and iron determination, to succeed at all costs in dominating the world in the coming century.

The British doctor and scientist Ronald Ross, who discovered the mosquito transmission of malaria (for which they won the Nobel Prize), was also a poet. On his return to India, where he had been born, after his qualification in London as a doctor, he wrote these melancholy lines:

Here by my lonely watchtower of the east
An ancient outworn race I see. . .

I don't think anyone would write this now, however true it might have appeared at the time to so intelligent a man as Ross. India, as Nehru put it, has awoken to new freedom, and the rest of the world has reason to take this fact's economic consequences seriously.

Ross's prejudice, however, was not incompatible with benevolence and humanity. On the day on which, after Herculean labors in conditions that would nowadays result in a lawsuit, he made the observation that established the mosquito transmission of malaria, he sat down to write another poem, much anthologized though often derided as mere doggerel:

I know this little thing
A million lives may save.
O Death, where is thy sting?
Thy victory, O Grave?

Tropical medicine in the colonial, or rather imperial context (there were never more than a few thousand British in British India), has often been regarded as but a further means of political control, but it is clear from Ross's poem that he did not think that his discovery would benefit mainly his own countrymen, and did not doubt that the saving of millions was a good thing. His prejudice did not preclude benevolence.

In my clinical work in England, I met large numbers of

patients who were either the victims or perpetrators of terrible cruelty. Of course, I had traveled in many countries that were in the throes of civil wars, and knew something of the inhumanity of man to man, but nothing had quite prepared me for the level of extreme violence in personal relationships that I encountered in a country that was enjoying sustained economic growth and unprecedented prosperity.

Certain policies of the state had contributed to the micro-Hobbesian world that I witnessed, for example, the welfare state's elimination of the very idea of desert when awarding benefits. But not even the most ferocious critic of such policies could claim that the behavior I witnessed was actually provoked, much less required, by the government. What I saw was human conduct as it becomes when the requirement to conform to inherited social restraints no longer exists, when it is left to the whim of individuals how to behave.

The result is an urban hell.

26 | The Dire Social Effects of Abandoning Certain Prejudices

OFTEN, as I have mentioned, I was consulted by women who had been abused by men. I do not mean a few such women, but thousands of them. I was also consulted by thousands of men who had abused women, and by not a few women who had abused men (by abuse, I mean violence that, committed in public, would, or ought to, result in prosecution and a jail sentence). I saw women who had been locked in cupboards or dragged down the stairs by their hair, or who had had the bones of their forearm "snapped," as they put it, or had been suspended by their ankles from tenth floor balconies.

It might be argued, of course, that this was nothing new: domestic violence, especially against women, is a human constant. An old Russian proverb suggests that a man who does not beat his wife does not love her (and it is the woman who quotes it). There is, I need hardly point out, an error of logic in the saying: it does not follow from the fact that if we beat only those whom we care about, then we do not care about those whom we do not beat. But at the other end of Europe, in England, there is a traditional rhyme to the effect that:

A dog, a woman, and a walnut tree,
The more you beat them the better they be.

The question, however, is not whether a phenomenon, for example burglary or murder, has always existed, but whether, even if it has, it has existed with greater or lesser frequency. And there is reason to suppose that the kind of violence whose victims and perpetrators I saw had increased, at least in Britain.

In the first place, the most common motive for it, nowadays at least, was sexual jealousy. With the breakdown of a socially accepted structure, or script, of relations between the sexes, this jealousy has itself increased very markedly, even dramatically. The idea, propagated by intellectuals who fretted at the frustrations of their own existence, as if such frustrations could be eliminated entirely from human existence, that, once free of all social obligations, contract, custom, economic considerations, sense of duty, and all the other factors "external" to them, relations between the sexes would be governed solely by mutual affection—which, if the latter waned (or waxed with a different object in view), would simply be amicably and rationally dissolved, without recrimination—was unrealistic, to say the least. It proved far easier in the event to remove sexual restraint than to overcome each individual's desire for the exclusive sexual possession of another; and it takes little effort of the imagination, even if we would rather not make it, to understand the result.

This is not to say that there was ever a time when there were no, or even few, sexual irregularities (our literature would have been very thin indeed without them), only that they had to be undertaken with discretion, with attempts to hide them. In these circumstances, sudden infatuations or irresistible lusts did not automatically deprive children of one of their parents, and could, when they were over, be allowed to recede into the mists of time. It was understood that feelings and inclinations were not always in lockstep with moral and social obligations.

The sexual revolution, after which everyone would supposedly be sexually fulfilled all the time, without a moment's respite, as it were, deprived people of this instinctive understanding, which had resulted from the operation of social prejudice on their minds in favor of the necessity of restraint. Instead, life was to be an open book, with nothing hidden from anybody. Furtiveness and its attendant dissimulation and hypocrisy were to be expunged from the human repertoire. Honesty and authenticity would be all.

The reality, at least in the area of the city in which I worked, was quite otherwise. The combination of sexual predation with an insistence on the fidelity of the current sexual partner has led to violence all round. Since we have a tendency to believe that the people around us are not so very different from ourselves, we are sexually predatory, we believe that such predation is the norm, and we see it practiced in the open; it is hardly surprising that we fall prey to the green-eyed monster, jealousy. No wonder that when another person happens to glance at our current "beloved" we should feel threatened; since prevention is better than cure, we give him a prophylactic punch in the face.

The violence is not gratuitous in the sense that it is without function, purpose, or rationale, even if it is not articulated. Let us leave aside the intrinsic joys and satisfactions of cruelty and brutality, which every boy who has ever plucked the wings from a fly (allegedly to find out something about its physiology) knows only too well; the domestic violence about which I learned in my medical practice had all the character-istics, except conscious thought, of a well-considered policy.

How does a man who lives in a sexual free-for-all, in which any casual encounter between a man and a woman may lead to a sexual liaison, bind a woman to him with hoops of steel, to ensure her fidelity? This is his problem, because he knows that his intrinsic charms, merits, and attractions are minimal, or at any rate, no greater than those of a thou-sand other men around him.

In these circumstances, it is best to fill his beloved's wak-ing hours with thoughts of himself and with nothing but thoughts of himself. If, after all, she is thinking of him, she cannot be thinking of the next door neighbor. Best, then, to deny her contact with other people, including her own fam-ily, and to telephone her all the time so that she knows she is under constant surveillance (what a boon are cell phones to the jealous!). He allows her out of the house only for mini-mal periods, and demands that she return by a time that is precisely fixed. Lateness by even a few seconds is an unfor-givable crime. He denigrates her and calls her ugly, so that she should consider herself lucky to have found so clever, strong, handsome, and protective a partner, willing to over-look her manifold defects. And finally, if this does not keep her in order, there is violence.

For maximum effect, there should be as little pattern to it as possible. It should be random, spontaneous, and insen-sate, and anything, even things that are the very opposite of supposed faults, should be capable of provoking it. In short, it should be arbitrary.

There are reasons for this. The arbitrariness is not itself arbitrary, for if it is, or appears, arbitrary, it can continue indefinitely. More importantly, if it is arbitrary, the victim will spend endless fruitless hours trying to work out what provokes the violence and how it may be avoided. This means that she will be preoccupied with him, to the exclusion of all else, which is precisely what he wants. The task he has set her—to work out a pattern where none exists—is intrinsically impossible; if she comes to any conclusion at all, it must be that there is something wrong with him, that he is ill, and therefore to be pitied rather than reviled, with a condition akin to epilepsy (though in fact there is often a pattern in the occurrence of seizures). If he is ill, he cannot, by definition, help himself; he needs help. As the victim says of him, "I think he needs help, doctor."

One of the interesting things about the perpetrators is that they often do not even try to conceal their character; indeed, they may even advertise it, at the very outset of their relationships. In many cases, it would be unnecessary for them to do so, for their reputation precedes them. For example, I was recently asked to prepare a medical report on a jealous man who had stabbed his lover nearly to death. In her written testimony, the victim said that, before she had ever gone out with him, she had heard bad things about him—namely that he was a violent, drunken, drug-taking criminal, with a history of beating women—but that she had accepted him into her life nonetheless.

His contrition for what he did, his avowed distress at his own behavior, his repentance after his violent outbursts, his promises not to do it again, his compensatory flowers and chocolates, and his search for medical assistance to "address his violence," as if he were the real victim, were part of the plan—if something not wholly conscious can be called a plan. His actions demonstrated to her that, in the inner core of his being, he was a good person, who would never have been a swine if something akin to an evil spirit did not periodically possess him and turn him into an evil bully. "When he's nice, doctor, he's very nice:" how many times I have heard that. If he were always nice, of course, she would have time to think of something, or worse still somebody, other than him; in the world in which victim and perpetrator live, he or she who commits adultery in his or her heart soon enough commits it in deed.

Reputation or not, such men do not deign to hide their character. They dress and comport themselves in an aggressive manner, and they may have themselves tattooed with the iconography of threat. If you saw them coming towards you in the twilight, you would cross to the other side of the street.

If what they are is written, sometimes literally, all over them, why do women take no notice of the signs? It is not that they are naïve or inexperienced, for many of them have experienced such men before (a few may think, as a result of their experience, that no other type exists). Leaving aside the excitement of danger, which at least preserves us from the horror of existential *ennui*, the answer given by many such women is that it would be wrong to jump to conclusions, to judge adversely, to stigmatize, or to stereotype.

They have accepted, perhaps without knowing it, the modern prejudice against prejudice, a prejudice that in their case might have preserved them from beatings and sometimes from death itself. The argument they have accepted goes something like this: the observation that men who dress and present themselves in a certain fashion and tattoo themselves heavily are bad men is at best a rough generalization, which is itself probably the result of class or ethical bias in the observer. Not *all* men who drink too much, that is to say, more than the Puritans who cajole and bully us, are bad men; therefore, man *x*, who drinks too much, is quite possibly not a bad man. One should not judge a book by its cover, they say (in my experience, not a wise saying even in a bookshop): to do so leads directly, by a short and slippery slope, to Auschwitz. The only ethical thing to do in such matters, therefore, is for a person to follow his or her own inclinations, that is to say, to have sex the moment it is offered, and not to pass judgment before the decision to live together. At least then the woman can be assured that she is not acting on a prejudice or being *judgmental*, even if it means a broken nose and permanently terrified children.

The Inescapability of
Commandments of Which
Justification Is Unprovable

THE NEED TO make up everything as you go along, to
accept nothing unless you can trace it to a first principle
that you yourself have discovered or invented, is the great
gift of the intelligentsia to the underclass. The results are not
difficult to imagine, but may be observed first-hand in many
places in the world, especially the rich parts of the world.

In practice, of course, it is difficult to accept absolutely
nothing on authority. The biologist Richard Dawkins, in his
book *The God Delusion*, quotes with approval one of the
new Ten Commandments with which a hopeful atheist
wants to replace the old Ten Commandments. Among the
new Commandments are: a) Test all things; always check
your ideas against the facts; and be ready to discard even a
cherished belief if it does not conform to them; b) Form
independent opinions on the basis of your own reason and
experience; do not allow yourself to be led blindly by others;
c) Question everything.

This has long been the supposed goal and role of intellectuals. The American black writer James Baldwin, in his
Fire Next Time, advises his nephew to "Take no one's word
for anything—even mine." This is a paradoxical injunction
that, if taken literally, would soon drive someone mad.

Does anybody live, has anybody ever lived, by these commandments? In the first place, there is an assumption that facts speak for themselves and will settle all questions worth settling, including those of belief. In fact, they will not even settle all questions of fact. It is a counsel of impossible perfection that people should believe things with precisely the degree of conviction that is warranted by the evidence that they themselves possess. Is there a single person in the history of the world, even the philosopher Bertrand Russell, a constant scold of convention, who has lived like this? I believe as strongly as I believe any historical fact that a battle took place in the vicinity of Hastings in the year 1066. I believe it so strongly because I have been told it all my life, it was the first historical date I ever learned, and no one has ever denied it. But if someone were to say to me, Prove to me that the Battle of Hastings took place in 1066, what would I answer? If I were to point to a secondary source, my interlocutor would answer, with justice, that I was arguing only from authority. If I then presented him with innumerable such sources, none of which contradicted the first source, he could still reply, and with justice, that mine is again an argument from authority, and that one does not check the accuracy of a story in *The New York Times* by buying another copy of the same edition. If I reply that the secondary sources are surely reliable, he will ask how I know that they are reliable, for it is a possibility that they are unreliable, all standing in apostolic succession, as it were, to an original error. According to the new Ten Commandments, I must question everything. If I do not, I am not a rational being, but a victim of prejudice and superstition.

Ah, I reply, I could check the secondary against the

primary sources. My interlocutor graciously consents to leave aside the question as to whether primary sources are always themselves reliable guides as to what actually happened, and how I distinguish those cases in which they are from those in which they are not; instead, he invites me to demonstrate to him by means of primary sources that a battle took place in or around Hastings in 1066. Actually, I can't do so, I reply; but I am confident that, if I devoted sufficient time to the development of the requisite skills, for example in reading documents of the time, I could do so, or at least push back the frontiers of my acceptance of authority. Of course, I am not actually prepared to do so, for it would take me the rest of my life merely to prove what I already knew—namely, that there was a battle at or around Hastings in the year 1066. But that is precisely my point, says my interlocutor, you know about the Battle of Hastings solely on the basis of authority, and you have failed to question everything, and you have failed to test your supposed knowledge by the light of your own experience and reason, and you have let yourself be led blindly by others. You are therefore culpably credulous; now let us move on to the Treaties of Nerchinsk and the Battle of Adrianople, and test the foundation of your supposed knowledge of them.

It would not, I think, be very difficult to prove that the great majority of our knowledge (or what the author of the New Ten Commandments might call superstition) is knowledge by authority. Would we really wish to be like the young denizens of the British slums who reply, when asked to name a British Prime Minister other than the current one and Mrs. Thatcher (even those suffering from Alzheimer's disease can remember Mrs. Thatcher), "I don't know, I wasn't born then"?

Would anyone suggest that medical students should recapitulate in their training the whole history of medicine and be required to demonstrate for themselves the truths of physiological science, which rest on an immense edifice of authority and sophisticated inference? Is it not one of the great glories of our civilization that a man of very moderate abilities may—perhaps must—know more than the greatest scientists and savants of the past? He sees further because he stands on the shoulders of giants, not because he has impertinently questioned everything they achieved. The average man in the street believes in the existence of viruses, and is right to do so, though if asked to prove their existence would not be able to institute a single line of inquiry leading to such proof.

A commandment, even of the kind propagated by Professor Dawkins, is a commandment, not an invitation to disputation. And if the majority of our factual knowledge of particular subjects is founded on trust and authority—for it is given to no man, however brilliant, to live long enough to be infinitely inquisitive—what of the dicta of moral and aesthetic judgment? I shall quote only what Hume said, for in my opinion he pointed to a difficulty that has not been satisfactorily overcome.

In every system of morality, which I have hitherto met with, I have always remark'd, that the author proceeds for some way of reasoning, and . . . makes observations concerning human affairs; when all of a

sudden I am surpriz'd to find, that instead of the
usual copulations of prepositions, *is* and *is not*, I met
with no proposition that is not connected with an
ought, or an *ought not*.

In other words, no statement of value can be derived in
logic from any statement of fact. There have been ingenious
attempts to demonstrate that Hume was mistaken, for
example, the purported demonstration by Professor Searle,
the American philosopher of language and mind, who is
undoubtedly one of the greatest living philosophers, that a
promise entails by definition an obligation. But can it really
be true that I ought to kill someone because, in a moment of
madness, I promised to do so?

28 | The Exercise of Judgment Unavoidable, Even in the Absence of Metaphysically Unassailable Principles, and Therefore Prejudices Necessary and Salutary

EVEN IF IT IS not possible to derive a statement of value from a statement of fact, it is nonetheless necessary and unavoidable that we make statements of value. We cannot live in a Gradgrindian world of facts alone. No one does or could take Mr. Gradgrind's injunction in Dickens' *Hard Times* as a blueprint for life:

> Now, what I want is facts. . . . Facts alone are what are wanted in life.

Of course, there are those who supposedly espouse non-judgmentalism as a philosophy, but they do so because they believe that they ought to do so, that is, they make precisely the kind of judgment that they claim not to make. The reason why they abjure such judgment is that the very word has now become synonymous, psychologically, if not yet in the dictionary sense, with intolerance and censoriousness, neither of them attractive qualities, particularly in a world in which people find themselves living cheek by jowl with many other kinds of fellow-humans. This gives rise to what one might call second-level censoriousness, or meta-censoriousness: that is to say, censoriousness about being censorious. (I shall never forget the beatific smile that played around a patient's mouth, like a breeze through corn, when I asked her to describe her own character: "non-judgmental," she replied, after searching for a short while in her vocabulary of self-praise. Moral complacency, oddly enough, is the natural consequence of non-judgmentalism as an ideal.)

In practice, however, no one lives or could possibly live without aesthetic and moral judgments of the kind that cannot be deduced from facts alone. It is a fact that the French-Swiss artist and architect Le Corbusier wanted to pull down the whole of the center of Paris in order to erect his simple geometrical shapes in Nuremberg-rally ranks (and he had the same plans for Buenos Aires and Rio de Janeiro); but if someone were to argue that what he proposed to build were superior to what he proposed to pull down, one could not point to any decisive fact or series of facts that would force such a person to withdraw or even reconsider. Whenever I say that Le Corbusier was one of the great monsters of the twentieth century, a century with a great deal of competition in that department, someone always pipes up that Baron Haussmann also laid waste to a lot of the Paris of his day. Yes, I reply, perhaps the good Baron did not have much regard for the wishes of many of the Parisians of his day, but he did not disrupt those lives for nothing. To this date, a flat that is in a Haussmannian building uses that fact as a selling point; would it ever have been a selling point of the Le Corbusian equivalent?

Good and bad, beautiful and ugly, are built into the very structure of our thoughts, and we cannot eliminate them

In Praise of Prejudice

any more than we can eliminate language, or a sense of time. Even the strictest Darwinian, of whom Richard Dawkins is perhaps the most forceful and eloquent representative, cannot avoid the realms of aesthetic and moral judgment. Dawkins writes clearly and sometimes elegantly; it is evident that he has chosen his words with great care. He might reply that he has done so simply because, as a matter of fact, clear and elegant prose persuades better than opaque and ugly prose; not only is this uncertain as an empirical observation (he himself is a ferocious and justified critic of a certain kind of French literary opacity that for a time was admired and aped throughout the Anglo-Saxon world), but it is untrue to his own obvious literary taste and erudition, in which he displays a deep feeling for the beauty of words. Again, he might argue that verbal fluency is a great advantage in finding a biologically superior mate, in the sense of one who would be most competent in the maternal tasks that ensure the preservation of a father's genes; but even this somewhat far-fetched explanation would not tell you whether Blake was a better poet than Byron, and why. Are the children of partisans of Blake at a survival advantage over the children of those of Byron? The fact is that the evolutionary explanation of the aesthetic faculty (I will not mention the bower bird in this connection) falls just as foul of Hume's objection as any other naturalistic explanation of aesthetic judgment.

And so it is with moral judgment, too. It may well be that the faculty of moral judgment has a satisfactory evolutionary explanation as to its development, but it cannot tell us very much about the individual moral judgments that we have to make every day. If biology explained morality, no two people in the same situation could come other than to the same moral conclusions. (And even if they were to, Hume's objection would still apply.) Dawkins' prose is, in fact, often filled with moral indignation: he thunders like an Old Testament prophet, though he rejects the model of the Old Testament God, not only on the grounds that he does not believe in Him, but for the same reason that John Stuart Mill, in his *Autobiography*, rejected him. Both writers depict this God as "sufficiently odious," that is to say, cruel and capricious, arbitrary and unjust, bad-tempered and unreasonable.

The Old Testament is full of the least edifying stories imaginable: heartless massacres and whole genocides in an apparent struggle—a Darwinian struggle, one might say—over resources. The New Testament represents an improvement, in Dawkins's view; but it is nevertheless flawed because it suggests that eternal damnation, in conditions far worse than those of a Nazi extermination camp, will be meted out to those who simply fail to believe correctly, a punishment grossly disproportionate to the crime, and one for which no further justification is given.

Unfortunately, no system of ethical propositions, or any other system of propositions, can exist without presuppositions, that is to say, prejudices. There is a point beyond which rationality, or naturalism, cannot go, even among creatures, such as my readers, who are endowed by nature with reason.

THE ATTEMPT TO pretend otherwise, however, deforms human character. Burke famously said that all that was necessary for evil to triumph was for good men to do nothing. (Note that he does not say that all men will become evil, only that evil men will become decisively powerful.) He might have added that evil would triumph if men ceased to believe in the distinction between good and evil, even if most of them continued in practice to behave tolerably well.

Why should this be? Let us consider a syllogism:

All prejudice is wrong.

The distinction between good and evil can be based only on prejudice.

Therefore, the distinction between good and evil is wrong.

Let us, however, consider a further syllogism:

The distinction between good and evil is both inevitable and necessary for the exercise of virtue.

The distinction between good and evil can be based only on prejudice.

> *Therefore, prejudice is necessary for the exercise of virtue.*

Which captures the real human situation better?

An effort to do the impossible—to expunge our minds from all preconception—is not merely doomed to failure, but affects our judgment in a baleful way. In order to prove to ourselves that we are not prejudiced, but have thought out everything for ourselves, as fully autonomous (if not responsible) human beings should, we have to reject the common maxims of life, common maxims that in many, though not in all, cases preserve civilized relations. Enlightenment, or rather, what is so much more important for many people, a reputation for enlightenment, consists in behaving in a way contrary to those maxims. And once a common maxim of life is overthrown in this fashion, it is replaced by another—often, though of course not always, a worse one.

I remember, for example, the occasion when a certain four-letter word was first used on BBC television. Contrary to what might be supposed, there was no public clamor on the part of angry proletarians that this ornament of speech should be employed over the air, in the name of gritty authenticity. It was, in fact, uttered by an Oxford-educated theater critic, Kenneth Tynan, for the very purpose of battering down what he thought were the imprisoning walls of verbal propriety, as if the English language, deprived of that word, were insufficient to express the deepest thoughts and emotions of humanity. Forty years later, we can see—or hear—the result. My next-door neighbor in France, who speaks no English at all, remarked one day to me that he was surprised to hear that word—the only one he knew in a language that boasts the largest vocabulary of any—always on the lips of the British who passed through that part of France. And these people, it should be remembered, were not the uneducated members of the underclass, to whom eleven years of compulsory attendance at school have imparted almost nothing except a hatred of anything but the fulfillment of their own immediate desires; these were middle-class people with very good jobs and incomes. It cannot, on the whole, be said that powers of self-expression, in the sense of the ability to communicate to others subtle thoughts and shifts of emotion, have been increased by the frequent resort to the use of this word, against which there was once a taboo; rather, the reverse has been the case. Nor would anyone expect that such powers of expression were proportional to the frequency of its employment.

The purpose of breaking the taboo was therefore not to achieve some worthwhile goal, such as the liberation of a part of humanity from obvious oppression, but to earn a reputation for moral and intellectual daring, by means of a triumph over prejudice and preconception. Only those with a prejudice against prejudice could have supposed that this represented in itself some kind of real advance.

But is it not also true that many prejudices are harmful, cruel, stupid, and vicious? Certainly it is. But I repeat, it does not follow that because some prejudices are harmful, we can do without prejudices altogether. All virtues carried to excess turn into vice, and become manifestations of spiritual pride; so it is with prejudices, even the best ones, and so it is with open-mindedness. I make no call never to examine our prejudices; such a call would be ridiculous. We need both the confidence to think logically about our inherited beliefs, and the humility to recognize that the world did not begin with us, nor will it end with us, and that the accumulated wisdom of mankind is likely to be greater than anything we can achieve by our unaided efforts. The expectation, desire, and pretense that we can go naked into the world, shorn of all prejudices and preconceptions, so that every situation is wholly new to us, is in equal measure foolish, dangerous, and wicked.

The pretense is harmful because we shall then deceive not only others, but ourselves, and disregard the still small voice within us. Shrillness and aggression will result. The more we insist in public upon things that we know, or even suspect, not to be true, the more intransigent and vehement we will grow. The more we reject prejudice qua prejudice, the harder it will be for us to retreat from the positions we have taken up in order to prove that we are not prejudiced. An ideological dogmatism will result, and we all know the havoc such dogmatism can wreak.

It takes judgment to know when prejudice should be maintained and when abandoned. Prejudices are like friendships: they should be kept in good repair. Friends sometimes grow apart, and so sometimes should men from their prejudices; but friendship often grows deeper with age and experience, and so should some prejudices. They are what give men character and hold them together. We cannot do without them.

Index

Acton, Lord, 45
Adrianople, Battle of, 116
Africa, writing a history of, 13
Alport, Gordon W., *The Nature of Prejudice*, 2
Argentina, natural resources in, 14
Asia, writing a history of, 13
Australia, historiography of, 13-15
Authority, attempts to dispose of, 47; knowledge dependent on, 48–49; resistance to, 100–103, 114–118
Ayer, A. J., 39

Bach, J. S., 103
Baldwin, James, *The Fire Next Time*, 114
Balzac, Honoré de, 14
BBC television, vulgarities on, 124
Bentham, Jeremy, 56
Berlinski, Claire, *Menace in Europe*, 8–9, 13
Blake, William, 121
Britain, Hindu immigrants in, 96–98; infant mortality rate of, 92; Sikh immigrants in, 96–98
Bunting, Madeleine, 36–37
Burke, Edmund, 123
Burundi, 2
Byron, George Gordon, Lord, 121

Cambodia, 93
Cameron, David, 51

Carlyle, Thomas, 55
Children, abandonment of, 81–82; education of, 17–18; selling junk food to, 18–20; sexual abuse of, 80–81
China, economic growth in, 11; prejudices about, 104
Class differentiation, 91
Coleridge, Samuel Taylor, 42
Columbus, 79
Communism, Soviet, 39
Consumer choice, 72
Custom, 57–59

Dawkins, Richard, 121–122; *The God Delusion*, 114, 117
Descartes, René, 6–7; *Discourse on Method*, 4–5
Dickens, Charles, *Hard Times*, 11, 119
Discrimination, 75–78

Education, 17–18
Egalitarians, 91–94
Engels, Friedrich, *Condition of the Working Class in England*, 11

Families, eating together, 21–22
Feet, on train seats, 63–67
Flaubert, Gustave, 34
Freudianism, 88
Funerals, proper attire at, 40–41

Index

Culture Counts has been set in Adobe Systems' Warnock Pro, an OpenType font designed in 1997 by Robert Slimbach. Named for John Warnock, one of Adobe's co-founders, the roman was originally intended for its namesake's personal use, but was later developed into a comprehensive family of types. Although the type is based firmly in Slimbach's calligraphic work, the completed family makes abundant use of the refinements attainable via digitization. With its range of optical sizes, Warnock Pro is elegant in display settings, warm and readable at text sizes – a classical design with contemporary adaptability.

SERIES DESIGN BY CARL W. SCARBROUGH